I AM
a Son

DESTINY IMAGE BOOKS BY DON NORI, SR.

The Forgotten Mountain
The Voice
Supernatural Destiny
Romancing the Divine
Manifest Presence
Breaking Generational Curses
Secrets of the Most Holy Place
Secrets of the Most Holy Place Vol. 2
Tales of Brokenness
The Angel and the Judgement
You Can Pray in Tongues
The Prayer God Loves to Answer
Breaking Demonic Strongholds
So You Want to Change the World?
How to Find God's Love
God: Out of Control, Out of the Box, Out of Time
No More Sour Grapes
The Love Shack
The Hope of the Nation That Prays
The God Watchers
Morning Prayer
God

I AM a Son

How Men and Women Become Mature Spiritual Sons of God

DON NORI SR.

Edited by Mercy Aiken

© Copyright 2017–Don Nori, Sr.

All rights reserved. This book is protected by the copyright laws of the United States of America. This book may not be copied or reprinted for commercial gain or profit. The use of short quotations or occasional page copying for personal or group study is permitted and encouraged. Permission will be granted upon request. Unless otherwise identified, Scripture quotations are taken from the New King James Version. Copyright © 1982 by Thomas Nelson, Inc. Used by permission. All rights reserved. Scripture quotations marked AMPC are taken from the Amplified® Bible, Classic Edition, Copyright © 1954, 1958, 1962, 1964, 1965, 1987 by The Lockman Foundation. All rights reserved. Used by permission. Scripture quotations marked AMP are taken from the Amplified® Bible, Copyright © 2015 by The Lockman Foundation, La Habra, CA 90631. All rights reserved. Used by permission. Scripture quotations marked ESV are taken from The Holy Bible, English Standard Version® (ESV®), copyright © 2001 by Crossway, a publishing ministry of Good News Publishers. Used by permission. All rights reserved. Scripture quotations marked KJV are taken from the King James Version. Scripture quotations marked NASB are taken from the NEW AMERICAN STANDARD BIBLE®, Copyright © 1960, 1962, 1963, 1968, 1971, 1972, 1973, 1975, 1977, 1995 by The Lockman Foundation. Used by permission. Scripture quotations marked NIV are taken from the HOLY BIBLE, NEW INTERNATIONAL VERSION®, Copyright © 1973, 1978, 1984, 2011 International Bible Society. Used by permission of Zondervan. All rights reserved. Please note that Destiny Image's publishing style capitalizes certain pronouns in Scripture that refer to the Father, Son, and Holy Spirit, and may differ from some publishers' styles. Take note that the name satan and related names are not capitalized. We choose not to acknowledge him, even to the point of violating grammatical rules.

DESTINY IMAGE® PUBLISHERS, INC.
P.O. Box 310, Shippensburg, PA 17257-0310
"Promoting Inspired Lives."
This book and all other Destiny Image and Destiny Image Fiction books are available at Christian bookstores and distributors worldwide.
Cover design by Eileen Rockwell
Interior design by Terry Clifton
For more information on foreign distributors, call 717-532-3040.
Reach us on the Internet: www.destinyimage.com.
ISBN 13 TP: 978-0-7684-3999-1
ISBN 13 eBook: 978-0-7684-4265-6
ISBN 13 HC: 978-0-7684-4013-3
ISBN 13 LP: 978-0-7684-4012-6
For Worldwide Distribution.
1 2 3 4 5 6 7 8 / 21 20 19 18 17

Contents

PROLOGUE   The Need to Know 1

CHAPTER 1   I AM a Son 5

CHAPTER 2   No Omen over Jacob 15

CHAPTER 3   A Prodigal's Paradise 25

CHAPTER 4   Father and Son 41

CHAPTER 5   No Other Way 53

CHAPTER 6   Two Sacrifices 65

CHAPTER 7   Maturing Sons 81

CHAPTER 8   Everything Else Is Less 95

CHAPTER 9   Sons Drink the Cup 107

CHAPTER 10 The Tell-Tale Disconnect 119

CHAPTER 11 So This Is Who I AM 129

CHAPTER 12 Jesus: The Pattern Son 139

            There Is No Last Chapter 159

Prologue

THE NEED TO KNOW

Who am I and why am I here? There are few things in this life I am desperate for, even fewer that I can't live without, and none that eclipses the need to know who I really am. Evolutionists say I am a freak of nature; the fact that I am breathing is one chance in billions. Theologians speak in deeply spiritual, unintelligible terms concerning the *whys* of existence. Apparently, the more confusing the speech, the more I should be fulfilled by it. But I no longer want to hear such lofty and empty language. I am finished with theories and ramblings of those who are devoid of experience, conviction, and inner character; who are guessing about almost everything they speak so confidently about.

I do not want to know "who the Bible says I am." I do not want to hear a preacher trying to explain who I am. I am not interested in what a philosopher, a professor, a doctrine, or a government says that I am. I want to know in the deepest belly of my spirit who I am, *really*, and why I am here.

I AM A SON

My search has been long and hard. No, it has been more than hard; it has been excruciating, terrifying, and often hell-bent. I have listened to the eloquent and simple, the refined and the base. I have given my rapt attention to the rich and famous, to the spiritual, the hermit, and the mystic. Each time, I walked away disappointed, with dashed hopes and broken expectations. All the assurances, testimonials, empirical evidence and promises were less than nothing in their ability to begin to touch me where I really live. Those who have influenced me (and there have been many) confirmed their words with the kind of love that encouraged me, opened the world to me, and were patient with me. If not for these authentic and loving shepherds, I am certain that my life would be quite different indeed.

I've sat with great men and cried with not-so-great men. I have helped the least with what the greatest demanded. I gave to the small what the powerful expected for themselves. I have been rejected by those whose love was confessed to be Divine. I have been told I was a great man by the same people who quickly took back those words when they realized that I would not be enamored with or bought by their flattery. I have looked in the high places for sincerity and often found only deceit. I have searched in the hallowed halls of exceptional sages only to find them a mere shadow of what they professed so powerfully to be before the masses.

I discovered that faith does not begin in a church, at a meeting, or "down the sawdust trail." Faith is not handed down from generation to generation, it is not available for purchase, nor is it reserved for mighty men of faith and power. I have found that greatness is within my arm's reach if I would be astute enough see it. I have discovered the most authentic, trustworthy, and loving place is not where most expect it to be and certainly not where the power hungry grovel and the proud pay their dues. Rather, it is only found within, where my Father, the King, has taken up residency and found His rest. I have felt the sweet embrace that can only be given by my Father. He holds me with an unconditional love that has convinced me in the deepest recesses of my heart that I AM His son.

No, I am certainly not much by the standards the world has set. Indeed, the desire for those accolades no longer holds me captive because I have already received the most incredible accolade a man could dream. I have found who I AM and I'm overwhelmed with the knowledge that I AM His son. This knowledge changes everything forever.

This is the story of what I have discovered in the daily experience of living—the crucible of life through the good times and the hard times, in times of ecstasy and times of near despair. Through it all, I discovered my beginnings and I found the path of my personal sojourn through this life. Of course, the days ahead will certainly bring a greater clarity concerning what I have already found. But that does not frighten me because I am on a journey of unfolding majesty, greater awareness of who I am and the synchronous union I have with my Father.

I am certain that some of what I write will comfort you, while other things will surprise you. Some will cause you to cry out for joy to your Father as I did when the reality of who I AM to Him and who He is to me began to dawn on my spirit. Certainly, some of what I write will be difficult to accept. Nonetheless, I am persuaded that the tangible reality of Who our Father is will cause the most resistant to release the binding shackles of mere humanity and begin to experience the wonders of being His son.

Chapter 1

I AM A SON

Writer's note: From a spiritual perspective, the term "son" is gender neutral. It is a spiritual reality of your Father's determined inheritance for you. To inherit the wealth of the family, you must be a son. In the Spirit, we are all sons—both male and female. We all have opportunity to inherit all our Father has for us. In exactly the same way, we are all the Bride of Christ, both male and female. These are spiritual terms to describe who we are in God using human language. Those willing to embrace these simple truths will experience Him in ways they cannot imagine. Behold, I AM a son; so are you.

My dearly beloved son,

There is more that you are intended to be than you can imagine. The key to this discovery is to be attentive to My Voice within rather than the voice of mere mortal men. There is more on My heart for you than you have been allowed to consider. But I am setting you free from the confinements of man. I want you to fly. I want your heart to soar. I want you to reconsider the things that man has told you are impossible. You are far more

> than you have become. If you can imagine it, your thinking is too small. It is time to simply, soberly, finally surrender to Me and allow yourself to dream and dream big. You are only a prisoner of another's smallness as long as you believe what they say. But I AM here to let you know that no matter what you have accomplished so far, you have barely begun. Open your heart, My dearly beloved son. Yield. Listen. Respond. As you do so, everything changes, beginning with you.

The Day Everything Changed

As usual, it was a busy day on that fateful afternoon in the lobby of Destiny Image Publishers. I had just completed a tour with a new author, introducing him to the folks he would soon be working with to turn his manuscript into a book. I took him from office to office, carefully showing him the steps to be followed and explaining the role that each person he was meeting would be playing in the process.

As we returned to the lobby where the tour began, my son, Don Jr., walked into the building. He was about to turn sixteen at the time, and had been homeschooled across my desk in my private office. Like my other sons, he had had the opportunity to work in just about every department in the building. Years earlier, he began sweeping floors, shoveling snow, counting books, and cleaning bathrooms. As he matured, he moved on to more critical roles in the company. At fifteen, the advantage of having been homeschooled next to my desk was becoming evident. It was clear that sons who grow up in the close company of caring, loving parents learn more and become more than can be imagined. All of our sons grew up close to us and were well-educated in the ways of the house (the business).

My son knew the drill. Knowing that we had an author coming in whom he had never met, he walked up to us with a big smile. Holding out his hand for an introductory handshake, he said, "Hi, I'm Don, welcome to Destiny Image."

The author looked at me and then back to him. "That's interesting," he said as he shook Don's hand. "You both have the same name."

An awkward moment followed as the author did not have a clue as to who my son was. "Yes, yes we do." Don said, smiling.

"So, do you work here? You look a little young."

"I do work here," was my son's reply.

"What is it that you do? Where is your office?"

Looking a little perplexed, Don told him he really didn't have a specific office.

Not to be put off, our guest persisted, "Really? You work here but don't have an office? Not even a cubicle? What is your job?"

Again a tad perplexed, Don looked at me and then back to our inquisitive guest. "I guess I do a lot of things," was Don's reply.

"You mean you work here but you don't know what you do?"

Humm, well, that required a bit of a deeper response. Don looked again at the guest, then to me and then back to the guest. With a big smile across his face and looking straight at me, he said, "Oh, I am his son. I do whatever Dad tells me to do. I'm in a lot of offices and in a lot of positions here. I can do whatever needs to be done."

As you can imagine, that conversation changed my life forever.

At that moment, a journey of incredible discovery began—one that has gone on now for 22 years. Everything I had ever seen in the Scriptures has been tested, scrutinized, and adjusted or destroyed by that one not-so-incidental conversation. I have painfully discovered that reality has a way of commanding our attention and demanding that we deal with it.

The Man-Appointed Gatekeepers

You know who they are. They are the religious, political, and economic rulers who control the systems of the world and, thus, control you and keep you in line with the "natural order of things." They try to keep humanity in lockstep with their view of how they want the world to be. Whether it be religious, political, economic, or cultural, these forces do not want free thinkers. They do not want their world invaded by the reality of God or by those who see what few others see. We can only be freed from their control when reality shakes up our world, our belief system, our life's plan. When the circumstances of life ruffle our feathers, we can be certain that those feathers needed ruffling. If we allow the ruffling, everything can change, something like scales falls from our eyes and we see more clearly than we had before. Foundational shifts in thought usually come with difficult circumstances. The deeper the difficulty, the deeper the change in thinking. Foundational revelation is only foundational if it can stand the test of fire—that is, the test of reality—which is the ultimate plumb line of our lives. This is the first and most important key to spiritual growth—what I believe must survive the fire or it is not worth holding on to.

Religion

For this book, my definition of religion is "the invention of man to justify one's actions and/or to subjugate those folks over whom spiritual truths are influential." The dimension of Spirit has power over the dimension where we live. If simple folks like you and I discover the latent power of the Spiritual dimension, the rulers of this natural dimension lose control. But make no mistake, the power we say we wield must be real power. It cannot be merely doctrine or theology. The power we say we have must work, and it must work outside the walls of a church and away from outdoor evangelistic meeting. The power that rules this dimension rules wherever it is used in a tangible, life-altering way. If it does not, the King and His Kingdom suffer marginalization as it has for the past two thousand years.

Without an authentic experience with God's love, it is impossible to give His love out to others. Rather, human effort is reduced to imitating the Divine (as if man can come close) and then is shocked, frustrated, and even angry when folks do not respond to their fleshy attempts to mimic what they do not have. This is what is typically called "religion" and is epidemic among believers. Although it is easier to pretend to have something you do not, reproducing Divine love is impossible when you have not experienced it.

What you sense within you concerning the heart of your Father is your greatest treasure. Even if it seems to go against accepted societal or religious norms, the true knowledge of Him is worth more than anything we might lose in the process. Your Father is the One within who is stirring your heart to listen more carefully, respond more obediently, and love more perfectly. That badgering witness in your heart, that churning in your stomach should not be ignored. You know the difference between last night's pizza and the Holy Spirit within. You know the difference between a bellyache and heartache.

Don't be afraid to buck "normal"! Of course, "normal" is subjective to the group using the word anyway. For our purposes, we are talking about the Christ-yielded lifestyle that oozes with all the attributes of our King. For those with the courage to respond to Him who speaks from within, you are in for the ride of a lifetime, a fulfillment that can be compared to nothing else and a destiny that only God could have dreamed up for you.

For all who are allowing themselves to be led by the Spirit of God are sons of God (Romans 8:14 AMP).

Our Greatest Testimony

"I AM a son" is a statement of identity and of Life. It is a declaration of destiny and empowerment, of love and of confidence. No testimony can be greater than the realization that above all else in life, I AM a son! That four-word declaration changes everything. It changes everything, that is, if I have experienced Him as my Father in the crucible of gritty circumstances and difficult people; the crucible of uncertainty and loneliness, loss and fear, despair and darkness. For those who are on the path of life, these are the instruments of transformational change that help us grow from a rebel son to a maturing son, from an immature son to a father. These unavoidable turns in life can certainly change us from whiners to doers, from takers to givers, from echoes to voices, from babes to kings who can co-rule with the King.

Of course, years of discovery are tempered with trials, mistakes, and struggles—the typical growing pains of a son maturing into adulthood. But one thing is for certain—once you know you are a son, no bump in the road can change that immutable fact. Participating in intense worship does not convince us that we are sons. It is not a revelation that is birthed in intercessory prayer or groaning in the Spirit. These are works of the Holy Spirit that will be common in the heart of a son, but they do not impart what can only be discovered. We must understand. This is not just another message for a Sunday morning or a Bible study topic. There is no pastor or prophetic word that can cement your genealogy in your heart. This identity is not inherited by a long line of preachers. Not even several generations of believers in the family can seal this deal.

Where, then, does the assurance of sonship come from? My spirit must touch His Spirit. Not in the usual Pentecostal ways I have just described, however. My spirit must touch His Spirit in the heart of calamity, failure, mistakes, and sin. As I run to my Father in my most desperate times of brokenness and confusion, heartache and uncertainty, separation and loneliness, He embraces me, forgives me, restores me, and heals my soul from the depths of sorrow and pain.

It is during these difficult times that I discover the unlimited power of my Father's unconditional, never-failing, always-healing love. I find Him truly, deeply in the valleys of deep, personal uncertainty. When I want to run, He runs beside me; when I want to die, He reminds me that He already did; when I want to quit, He holds me up. It is then I discover what it means to be a son of my Father who, truly, will never leave me, forsake me, or lose hope in me.

I know I AM a son because my Father proved Himself when I needed Him most. He never doubted, never gave up on the dream He has for me, never lost confidence that I would fulfill my destiny. This is the knowledge that a Bible school can't teach, a prophet can't declare, a worship song can't impart, and decreeing can't force. I AM a son because I run to Him every day without excusing my humanity, blaming someone else or whining over an unfair circumstance.

With full knowledge that there is nowhere else to run, nowhere else to hide, no one who can pardon as He pardons or gather has He gathers, I run confidently to Him. He embraces me, holds me, and calls me His own. I don't need a special definition of grace. I don't even need a dose of "extravagant" grace. I only need Him, Whose Fatherly embrace convinces me more deeply every moment that I AM His son. When no one else understands, no one cares, when everyone else runs from me, He is there. He is within, without, around, and resting in my heart telling me again and again, "You are My son." Yes, in Egypt I found Him my Deliverer. In the Wilderness, I discovered Him my Provider. But in Canaan, I have found Him my Father.

The Experience of Sonship

I am not afraid to tell anyone who I am or what I have experienced. I don't merely hope to attain my place as a son—because in Christ I already have it. Faith is the substance things I have hoped for (see Heb. 11:1). I have the knowledge of daily experience with Him. I love talking with Him, sensing Him within and listening to Him encourage me, teach me, and direct me. I have come to the point where I cannot do anything unless I know I am hearing Him. I can no longer flippantly say, "I heard God's Voice," "I was led by the Spirit," or "I have a prophetic word for you." These things are just too precious to be cheapened by such fleshy antics. If I have heard from Him, there will be a response within the person or people to whom I speak. That is what should tell anyone whether I have heard from God. That inner witness confirms His word to the heart and urges the hearer to pay attention.

My Father is alive! He is within me. He is beside me, in front of me, behind me, over top of me, and beneath me. He hears. He knows. He understands my motives, plans, and desires. I am an open book before Him. I am absolutely transparent before Him. I can hide nothing. I cannot say what He is not saying or do what He is not doing. Sons moving toward their Father's heart leave the elemental things of the world, of spiritual infancy, behind to pick up the reality, the responsibility of mature sons.

Of course, the implications of this experience are far-reaching and cannot be covered in one short chapter. But rest assured that we have barely begun to understand, let alone experience all God has prepared for those who love Him. Nevertheless, He is revealing them to us by His Spirit. For those hungry enough for Him, frustrated enough with what is, tired enough of the monotony of rote religion, even Pentecostal/Charismatic religion, a whole new Day is dawning. A New Song is being sung. I hear it clearly in my spirit: "I AM a son!"

The Discovery of the Ages

Many years ago, my son discovered the power, the benefits, the opportunities, and the responsibilities of being a son. In the course of his daily interaction with me, our relationship grew and flourished. He *grew* into what he was *born* into because he stayed in authentic, dynamic friendship with his dad. He became what destiny had written on his heart. *"Oh, I am the son. I do whatever Dad tells me to do,"* he said to the visiting author. He was more than just a biological son. He had become a son after the heart of his father.

> *Jesus gave them this answer: "Very truly I tell you, the Son can do nothing by himself; he can do only what he sees his Father doing, because whatever the Father does the Son also does"* (John 5:19 NIV).

Let us not be content with being a babe in Christ, a rebelling prodigal. Let us live in brokenness and surrender so that we might grow into our true destiny as functional kings, maturing sons of our Father.

Compelling Questions for Maturing Sons

1. Do you feel the churning within you for something more? How have you responded to it?

2. Is it easy for you to run to your Father when you feel broken and hurting? What about when you sin and fail? Why?

3. What do you see the Father doing? Are you doing it with Him? Are you allowing Him access to your life that He may make you into a son who can work with your Father?

Chapter 2

NO OMEN OVER JACOB

> My dear son,
> It will always be easier to cry in your soup than it is to accept that you are still mortal. I know, I know. The promise is not a promise to struggle. But it's a process—a process intended not only to change you but to keep you humble, teachable, softhearted, and compassionate. Giving you the power to live perfectly without allowing the time for your mind to be transformed is a tad reckless, don't you think? In the meantime, I have your back. Stay repentant, attentive. Resist arguments with yourself and trust your "now" to the only One who can make it glorious. Look up—amazing things are happening. You win.

"I AM a son." There is no phrase more comforting, no truth more compelling, no title more honorable. There is no reality more life-changing, no word more powerful, no position more final. There is no phrase more empowering than the truth of these four little words: "I AM a son!"

These simple words can ensure your future and convince you of your Father's intent. They can give confidence where there is uncertainty, hope where there is despair, and an identity that can never be stolen. "I AM a son!"

Our Father has always loved His sons. He has always been very protective over them, reassuring them of His faithfulness. He is confident of His own ability to fulfill His dream for them. He spoke through prophet after prophet, epoch after epoch, encouraging, directing, disciplining, and calling His sons to Himself.

When Balak was determined to destroy his enemy Israel, he called Balaam to come curse him. But try as he might, he could not curse whom God had blessed. He could not curse the one upon whom destiny was set. He could not curse Israel, the son whom the Father had determined to love. No, Balaam had to go back to Balak with the news that would ensure the fulfillment of Israel's destiny, the protection of Israel's future, the salvation of Israel's soul through the Christ Who would come through her.

"There is no omen against Jacob, nor is there any divination against Israel," Balaam declared to the king of Moab (see Num. 23:23). That statement rings powerfully through the ages to this present time. There is no omen, no curse, no determined effort that can succeed against His sons, because our Elder Brother has already triumphed for us all. Our Father is at work for His good pleasure within and among maturing sons who bear His Name. Through Christ, He has defeated the work of the enemy that raged against His own. Isaiah saw this when he wrote:

> *"Comfort, O comfort My people," says your God. "Speak kindly to Jerusalem; and call out to her, that her warfare has ended, that her iniquity has been removed, that she has received of the Lord's hand double for all her sins." A voice is calling, "Clear the way for the Lord in the wilderness; make smooth in the desert a highway for our God. Let every valley be lifted up, and every mountain and hill be*

made low; and let the rough ground become a plain, and the rugged terrain a broad valley; then the glory of the Lord will be revealed, and all flesh will see it together; for the mouth of the Lord has spoken" (Isaiah 40:1-5 NASB).

Our Warfare Has Ended

I have stopped living as though the devil is chasing me, nipping at the heels of my shoes. I have stopped with the endless tirade of rebukes and decrees. I am done with living in a state of continual warfare all in the name of trying to lessen the influence and impact of the enemy of my soul. I have come to see that satan is not deserving of all the attention I had once given him. Back then, I lived as though I was on an African safari looking to kill the king of the jungle. I had not yet realized that my King is already the authentic and reigning King of everything, every nation, every world, every dimension, every universe. I do not have to hunt down an enemy already destroyed or try minimize the so-called influence of him who has no authority or right over my life. I spent too many years looking for a shelter from this evil one only to realize that I AM the shelter over the influence of the enemy. I AM the high tower that others can run to that I may introduce them to Him Who covers them in the shadow of His mighty wings. I know who I AM in Christ. I AM a son.

I have discovered, once and for all, that there is no omen against me, just as there is no omen against my Elder Brother, Jesus. There is no divination at work against me, because there is none at work against Him. I can no longer use that excuse for my troubles, temptations, and tears. My war is over because He finished it. My Elder Brother took satan by the throat and destroyed His influence in my life when He was nailed to the Tree. The simple truth—that there is no omen against us, first spoken by a diviner hired to curse Israel—should be shouted from the housetops. It should be splattered with Blood on the doorposts of every man's heart, written into every song we will ever sing, every book we will ever read for it is the monumental triumph of King Jesus for His family, you and I. He did what Isaiah said needed to happen. The playing field has been made level, the stones of stumbling have been removed, and the Wilderness has been turned to a broad plain. Our King Jesus, our Firstborn Brother, was the first to walk the way of salvation on this earth. He did what is not only possible but is intended for us in this life. I know who HE IS—the victorious Son. Therefore, I know myself. I AM also His son.

The manifest victory of the Risen Christ of God is now prepared for those who will walk on that same highway of holiness, where God has come with vengeance in His destruction of the enemy and satan's now-defunct strongholds. When He ended the reign of satan's terror, our King did what no man could do. In three days, He did what the entire nation of Israel could not do in thousands of years. No wonder Isaiah saw the redeemed of the Lord returning to the King with a shout of victory, with everlasting joy in their hearts and minds. The redeemed have found gladness and joy. Sorrow and sighing are a thing of the past. And no wonder! They are His sons!

At long last, sons have safe passage on a road where the unclean will not travel, where fools will not wander and where no lion patrols. Nothing evil is able to tread upon it. No vicious beast will be found there because it is the Blood-conquered highway upon which only the King and His redeemed may walk.

On this manifestly victorious highway of life, those who were blind now see the glory of the Father within their hearts. The hearing-impaired can listen to the joyful sound of salvation. King Jesus, our Firstborn Brother, has delivered us. He has given us peace within. He has given us Himself. He has commissioned us to be carriers of His Life,

His love, His predictable attributes, and His power. The lame leap, the mute hear, the joy of the Lord flows from their hearts like rivers in a desert, for He has done the impossible. He has put us on the highway cleared by the King Himself. Humanity now has a new hope. Anyone who is willing can walk on this road constructed by the determined love of our Father, a road that clears away the work of the enemy of our soul. This enemy was once and for all time humiliated by the resurrected Conqueror, the Firstborn Son, who could not be contained by the rants and commands of a defeated opponent. This path of victory is for us to experience in this life; it has been prepared for all those who love Him.

The Other Side of the Story

So, if there is no omen against me, no divination over me, why do I struggle so much? Why is it that I don't see this reality in my everyday life? The answer is simpler than it is palatable. Ever since Adam blamed Eve for his disobedience, man has been shifting blame, refusing responsibility and justifying his own actions. Blame-shifting is so ingrained in us that we do it without thinking. We blame-shift to deflect the real reasons we find ourselves falling short of God's glory. But, surprisingly, there is remarkably good news in all of this—a way out of the vicious cycle of blame and shame.

I have made a new confession for myself: It is not my wife in need of prayer and repentance. It is not those nasty politicians or the mainstream media who are to blame. I cannot kick the dog, throw out the cat, blame the weather or my arthritis. It is I, Lord, standing in need of authentic repentance and prayer for transformation and the strength to go on. Even if I must confront my weakness every day, I refuse to make an excuse for it. I will not create a doctrine that makes it OK to do the stupid things I do. There is only one escape from this mess. There is only one path to maturity, only one heartfelt prayer that sets me free: "I repent." In fact, according to Jesus, repentance is required in order to partake of His Kingdom:

> *From that time Jesus began to preach and say, "Repent [change your inner self—your old way of thinking, regret past sins, live your life in a way that proves repentance; seek God's purpose for your life], for the kingdom of heaven is at hand"* (Matthew 4:17 AMP).

Repentance changes everything. It releases chains of guilt and frustration. It blows away the darkness that tries to cloud my vision, skew my determination, and weaken my resolve. *"I repent"* is the roadway to union with my King, to the fulfillment of my soul's deepest desire.

Authentic to the Bone

At some point in my journey, I found that only by being authentic to the bone would I ever be able experience the union with the King that I wanted so much. I had watched countless folks make incredible confessions, pronounce vows of brotherhood, confidentiality, and commitment to my well-being. I have been given countless promises that did not survive the fires of the daily tumult. I have experienced countless broken contracts, promises ignored, and squandered trust. Whilst reeling in one of these unexpected situations, I came to the realization that I could not trust *anyone*. I know, I know. You can throw a dozen scripture verses at me showing me where that's not supposed to happen. But that is exactly the point. It did happen and it does happen—again and again. These are the cold hard facts of life in the world and the religious system. Don't make the mistake of trying to call this sort of behavior the Church Jesus is building. It isn't.

Because of this, Isaiah's "highway of holiness" looks more like the torture chamber from hell. The roadway of religion is littered with broken hearts, broken souls, and the broken dreams of countless millions who opened themselves to someone they thought they could trust and were summarily burned, broken, and bruised by them or their organizational minions. And it was all done in the name of love, no less. No wonder Jesus said that He did not entrust Himself to anyone (see John 2:24).

Obviously, this is not Isaiah's "highway of holiness." The highway that he saw was much different, indeed.

> *A highway will be there, and a roadway; and it will be called the Holy Way. The unclean will not travel on it, but it will be for those who walk on the way [the redeemed]; and fools will not wander on it. No lion will be there, nor will any predatory animal come up on it; they will not be found there. But the redeemed will walk there. And the ransomed of the Lord will return and come to Zion with shouts of jubilation, and everlasting joy will be upon their heads; they will find joy and gladness, and sorrow and sighing will flee away* (Isaiah 35:8-10 AMP).

Where evil things are happening, our King has no authority in the hearts of the people because they are not in His Kingdom. It is not authentic sons who come to kill, steal, and destroy, but the enemy of our soul—our fleshy anti-Christ nature.

These painful experiences put me in the position of judging myself. As I observed others hurting folks, I began to review all the times I was the one doing the injuring. What the King showed me broke my heart. I wept. I repented. I determined that, although I could not force others to act according to the nature of the King who lived within them, I could at least commit myself to treat others as I wanted to be treated. From that point on, and by the grace of God, I would surrender my thoughts, my imagination, and my tongue to Him Whose ways are far higher than mine. I would surrender my human right to be a fleshy, self-centered hypocrite. And He would most certainly transform my life into one most reflective of His Life and love. He is still doing it.

Authentic believers do not simply confess with their mouths. They change. They expect the King to work within them. They expect life's trials to bring confrontations to their humanity so that they can see themselves in their fleshy reality as it exists apart from their Father. Many say a short prayer of repentance after sinning so as to mellow their conscience for a few hours. But heartfelt repentance is a determination to change, an expectation that the King will authorize, initiate, and complete the change once we open the door to it by simply admitting that we have sinned and then yielding to His transforming powers.

The prayer of a true son is, "Create in me a clean heart, O God, and renew a steadfast spirit within me" (Ps. 51:10).

Swallowed Up with Life—Now

Those who are courageous enough to believe these words will find themselves exactly where they need to be in order to begin to experience this otherworldly, Christ-infused lifestyle. Because all the roadblocks have been taken away, there leaves none to accuse and no one to blame. For if the truth be told I am the stumbling block to the fullness of union with God I so desperately want to have. Until my mortality is swallowed up with Life, I will always have this irritating, moment-by-moment struggle with the things that distract, confuse, accuse, tempt, and otherwise frustrate me beyond anything I can think of. But these things are merely the mortal man passing away as the Life consumes the old Don. Sometimes I wonder how He can continue to be so patient with me as I waddle through this life with the DNA of His Son, a King by decree, a priest in Order of Melchizedek, an ambassador by appointment, and yet still struggle with this mortal, rebellious flesh nature. And yes, sometimes my seeming lack of progress really depresses me.

Nonetheless, I am His son. I may not be yet what I want to be. I may not see myself the way He sees me, but my confidence is that He is most definitely at work within me, constructing the place He calls home and sitting on the throne of my heart, which He has dubbed, "the Mercy Seat." You see, I may not see everything under His feet yet, but I see my King, I see Jesus, who is determined to fulfill the dream He has dreamed for me. All He really needs is my cooperation to see it come to pass. I have full confidence, full expectation that His Life will swallow up mine, that His Life will be clearly seen in me, through me, and sometimes in spite of me as I live softly, circumspectly before my Father.

The path before us is the path to victory, never failure. Should we continue on it, it is the path that will bring us to the place of mature sonship. We will become those with whom our Father will entrust with the secrets of His eternal Kingdom. The way is not overwhelming; it is not for a carefully selected few. It is for all who will patiently take the path forward one step at a time.

Let us be brave. Let us be determined. Let us walk in the path that is marked by His very footsteps. There is no omen. There is no curse. This pre-determined path does not end in failure. The enemy of our soul is defeated. It is the human side of us that is the issue—our ego that blames the devil and everyone else for our issues and failures. It is amazing the freedom that we can experience when we simply admit our own fault. Taking personal ownership for sin is the only first step to final deliverance from the stuff we all hate, the stuff that keeps us short of His glory within. "He must increase. I must decrease!" This confession is an exhilarating trumpet call from deep within that says to this dimension and any other dimension that is listening, "I AM a son!"

Meditations for a Maturing Son

1. Is repentance part of your daily lifestyle? Are you allowing your King to show you where you must change? Are you resisting the urge to blame another? Why or why not?

2. Do you see that "no omen over Jacob" applies to you? Can you accept the forgiveness of your King and go on or do you need time to "get over" what you have done? Do you know the guiltless feeling of walking on the path where no lion intrudes?

3. Do you believe that in Christ you have a right to abide in such a place? If so, does this change how you will live today?

Chapter 3

A Prodigal's Paradise

The younger of them [inappropriately] said to his father, "Father, give me the share of the property that falls to me." So he divided the estate between them. A few days later, the younger son gathered together everything [that he had] and traveled to a distant country, and there he wasted his fortune in reckless and immoral living.
—Luke 15:12-13 AMP

My dear son,

    There is no doubt that I have a plan. It is awesome but not automatic. It is destined but not determined. Your cooperation, your surrender every day is the ultimate determination as to whether or not you experience the dreams I have for you. But I am confident; be at peace. I AM happy that you are giving yourself to surrender, even in the things you don't want to give up. That *is* the growth process. Transformation is the path to maturity, fulfillment, joy. When ancient Israel was to leave Egypt, a lamb had to be sacrificed. For you to be freed from the bondage of sin, the Lamb of God had to be sacrificed. So

> now, for you to leave the Wilderness, that aimless and poverty-stricken way of life, you become the sacrifice. You must die to yourself and the wanton sin that overcomes you. You must give up the Wilderness thinking that keeps you from fully experiencing all I have for you. Trust Me. Keep surrendering. Repent. Change. Grow. Listen to the sound of My Voice. When you do, everything changes and you most certainly win.

Everybody wants to be a "mature" son. Everyone wants the inheritance coming to them as soon as possible. Some go so far as to demand it before the appointed time. Think of this young man—an immature son but a son nonetheless. He was so self-absorbed that he wanted to take his share of the inheritance without considering what it would mean to the rest of the family. He didn't consider the family's ability to run their business without the portion demanded by his whining demands. All he knew was that he wanted what was coming to him—*now*.

Little did this young man realize that his inheritance was far more than what he could see. His inheritance was far more than what he could stuff in his pocket. He stood to reap a maturity, a development of character, a "becoming" that would not only give him wealth for the present but wealth for his children for generations to come. His father would give him wisdom, authority, and honor for the rest of his days. Consider how growing, maturing with his father would give him the tools that would cause his life to blossom. One the one hand, he could recklessly grab what was rightfully his and waste it in a short amount of time. But the wealth given him was intended to—through proper investment, proper management, proper personal control of his desires—produce a lifetime of security and prosperity, as well as an inheritance that he could then pass on to his own children. Instead, he chose to squander it on his own selfishness and personal lusts, leaving nothing for his future.

Consider authority. Contrary to popular belief, authority cannot be assigned. It cannot be truly delegated. It cannot be bought. True spiritual authority can only be earned through personal trials and storm. One does not simply get solutions to hard times by reading a book. Answers come through humbling ourselves, allowing the Holy Spirit and sometimes others to instruct, direct, correct, and even admonish us. But make no mistake, I am not talking about submitting to overlords who have the power to tell us what to do but have no authentic relationship or friendship with us. Only when we are absolutely convinced that someone has our best interests at heart can we safely listen carefully to what they have to say. This kind of trust cannot be assigned or directed. It is not earned by listening to a sermon every week or sitting in a Bible study. This kind of trust happens as people walk together, work together, see each other as peers. This is true brotherhood; this is family. These are the relationships of sons to fathers or siblings to siblings.

Consider respect. Respect does not come when we throw a few letters before or after our name. A title or position does not automatically give us heart-earned respect. Our bank account, the size of our house, or a particular talent or gift does not earn the kind of respect that will cause another to be vulnerable to us, trust our words, or allow us access to his deepest issues of life. Respect is the product of years of observation, truthfulness, faithfulness, humility, and servanthood. Respect is an attribute that is earned in the crucible of sharing troubles and hard times together. It finds a place to flourish in the resulting love and personal care one for another. Whether in words or actions, respect, once earned, is a priceless and cherished gift we share with each other through our actions, our kindness, and authentic, non-judgmental love.

I AM A SON

It's a "Family Thing"

When my sons come for dinner now as adults, they sit around the table as they always have. They do not sit in their titles and positions they hold away from the table. They sit together as sons at the table of their parents. Their positions and titles mean nothing around this table. They are united; they are one as the Nori sons, each with a special set of tools in their business, personal, and ministerial lives. They demand no positional respect, no professional title, no special authority at that table. But they are comfortable to be peers around a table that is collectively more powerful than they are individually.

They are smart enough to know this. They are respectful and wise enough to understand the honor of the seat they have where they are fully accepted for who they are. Seated at the table of their nurturing, they find the peace that gives them clarity of thought, the acceptance that gives them courage to attempt the impossible with permission to fail, the power to explore the unknown frontiers of their journey. The love they share keeps them close. The grace they feel keeps them humble. The possibilities of the table itself keep them imagining things that can be dared no other way. This is the true body politic of our faith at work. This is the essence of body life. It is the precise opposite of what most believe about "the body" today.

The table of peers brings mutual respect, camaraderie, a distinct absence of vitriolic competition. Rather, an atmosphere of growth and discovery is nurtured, leading to a Divine lifestyle of transformation, one that they will embrace for the rest of their lives. Yes, around that dinner table, there are only sons. The conversations inspire, encourage, strengthen, and sometimes challenge. There is joy and hope. The atmosphere is always charged with possibilities. There's no vying for attention or control, no proving of who they are. They are already the most they can be around this table. They are sons.

Over the years, Cathy and I have had the honor of hosting some very awesome people around our table from ministry and business, although there is no difference between the two in God's eyes. Dr. Myles Munroe, Dr. Patricia Morgan, Dr. Kelly Varner, Mahesh and Bonnie Chavda, The Arnotts, Dr. Kingsley Fletcher, Sam Houston, Peter Whyte, Dr. Mark Hanby, Dale Rumble, Cleddie Keith, Scott Willis, Don Milam, Alan Knight, Reuben and Lacy Egoff, as well as ambassadors and presidential candidates. Yet, as we sat together, there was something far more special at work than ministry. We sat together as sons. We sat at a table that no man had set, no man tried to control, and no man cared to leave. Such are the times of authentic sons. Such are the meetings of those who have been gathered together by sacrifice—their own.

I AM a Son

My Father is Divine in nature and His offspring are like Him, created in His image. One cannot be a son of God and be merely a flesh-and-blood humanoid. Paul entreated us, "Quit you like men" (1 Cor. 16:13 KJV). We are more than we realize. Something far greater than our religiously determined limitations is at work here.

Like my Elder Brother, Jesus, I AM a person who is 100 percent man and filled with a Sprit who is 100 percent God. Nevertheless, my experience is far, far less than the reality that is truly me. Because of this very prevalent attitude, it is difficult to soar the way were created to soar. Because we see ourselves as far less than God's determined expression within us, most reject not only Who truly indwells us but our fitfulness to even contain the purity of the Divine. But that is just the reason for the work of Jesus on the Cross. His death and resurrection cleansed the Throne Room of our hearts that He might take up permanent residence there. For me, the argument of the permanence of my salvation is completely moot. Those who make such distinctions do not see the bigger picture of Who He is and what He wants to do through the likes of simple folks like you and I. The question is not, "Can I lose my salvation?" The question is, "Will I surrender to Him so that the fullness of the Godhead can be expressed through me as He lives in me?" The extent to which the Divine is expressed in me, through me is directly proportional to the yieldedness of my heart. No, I am not perfect. No, I have not yet conquered all my imperfections. But I see my Elder Brother who lives within. He is the initiator and finalizer of my faith. I trust Him to bring forth all of His good purposes in me and through me. In our redemption and restoration, He will prove—in us—the power of the Cross.

Our journey mirrors the journey of the Ancients. It will culminate in the visible expression of His Kingdom in us and through us. Like the Ancients who focused everything outward—on the pillar of smoke and fire, the manna and the quail, the water that flowed from the Rock—most of us are too focused on the outward man as well. The decisions we make, the hope we carry, and the faith we maintain are based on the input we receive from the five senses. Our impressions are based on the natural with little or no spiritual input. We have become so accustomed to the input from the natural five senses that we inadvertently ignore what our spiritual senses are trying to convey to us. It is no wonder that a constant faith is so hard to live when there is no constant input from spirit to Spirit within.

When we begin to refocus on being led by the Holy Spirit within us, our decisions now have the additional input of God. Our growth is determined to the extent we give ourselves to hear from our Indwelling King rather than the human senses of the natural man. Our maturity is ultimately determined by who we surrender to—either to Him and our spiritual senses or to ourselves and the human senses that send information to the soul without the benefit of any input from Spirit.

Yes, I AM a son. I AM human and I AM Divine. Only tomorrow will witness what we will do with the Living Christ within, as He is released through otherwise ordinary folks. But now, as far as it is up to me and as far as I can access His mighty grace, I walk with dogged determination, Divine anticipation, and unwavering assurance that He who began a good work in me will complete it, regardless of how others have settled for far less. The good work He is doing is not merely keeping me for heaven. It is not maintaining just an outward appearance of holy living. This work of God is nothing less than the 100 percent man yielding to the 100 percent God who indwells him so that the world may know through tangible, physical demonstration in time and space that my Father has sent His Son to redeem, establish, and expand His mighty rule and reign in the earth—my earth first and then all of creation.

Sons Transcend Position

Sons transcend the house, the work of the house, the positions of the house, the authority of the house, and the destiny of the house. For truly, sons are the manifest destiny of those who make up the house. Titles are merely subsets of "sons." A son has the run of the house. He can do anything that needs to be done, be trusted with anything of importance, sent on any mission, and rule in any situation. Cathy and I have raised five sons. We wanted them to have a heart of a servant, which they do. Yet, they are more than servants. We wanted them to be our friends, and they are. But they are more than friends. We wanted them to walk with God, and they do. But they are more than disciples. They represent their King before man, but they are more than ambassadors. They are my *sons—my offspring, bone of my bone and flesh of my flesh.* Of all the men who inhabit the earth today, they alone are my sons. In my eyes, there is no fact about them that is stronger than this core aspect of their identity.

Of all the titles we can achieve in life, the most compelling is the name that recognizes our beginnings and our destiny. Of all the accolades that the world or religion can bestow, there is one that I cherish above all of them. I AM a son.

An Ugly Spectacle

Behold, what manner of love the Father hath bestowed upon us, that we should be called the sons of God: therefore the world knoweth us not, because it knew him not. Beloved, now are we the sons of God, and it doth not yet appear what we shall be: but we know that, when he shall appear, we shall be like him; for we shall see him as he is. And every man that hath this hope in him purifieth himself, even as he is pure (1 John 3:1-3 KJV).

There was an unfathomable price paid for us to receive the privilege to call ourselves "sons." It is here that we make up the sufferings of Christ and begin to understand, howbeit in small measure, what our King suffered for us. The Cross was an ugly spectacle, where our Lord was put on display for the world to see. It was the terrifying price our King paid for our benefit alone to eradicate sin. No, the Cross was not wonderful, it was not sweet, and it was certainly not a sight that any sane person could love. The Cross, in its evil finality, is nothing to be embraced. But it is the path of true resurrection, and Jesus calls us to carry it, even as He did. He was not referring to putting a cross on a chain around our necks. The cross we bear is the cross of suffering and death in order to do the will of our Father, just as Jesus did and now paves the way for us to do the same.

And he said to them all, If any man will come after me, let him deny himself, and take up his cross daily, and follow me (Luke 9:23 KJV).

Our cross is as deadly as His was deadly. It is as final as His was final. It is as repulsive as His was repulsive. It is as eternally transforming as His is to this day. It is as required as His was required. Human attempts to "beautify" the depraved process of human crucifixion are a travesty at best and Divine humiliation at worst. You just can't dress up what happened to Him. You just can't make it less horrific than it was. It is no wonder that contemporary Christianity has turned so soft, so clean, so professional. Authentic Resurrection, like our King's, must be preceded by authentic crucifixion, like our King's. He agonized for six hours, refusing to call in His angelic armies to free Him. He bled, anguished, and finally suffocated in intolerable pain for the likes of me. No wonder so many want to make that moment in history less offensive. If His suffering wasn't so bad then neither should we have to suffer so. My goal should not be to run from the Cross, not to rebuke, ignore, deny pain or suffering. It should be to fall in surrender before the King in order that I might hear His Voice. But that is surely not the path of most of us. We would have called in those angelic armies! Like Peter, we would have drawn our swords in the Garden. Most believers would never believe that God could intend them to suffer even remotely as Jesus suffered. Most would have been crying out for deliverance in a moment of time, totally missing the point of death. Had Jesus called on His delivering legions or allowed Peter to choose the path of earthly violence, as ridiculous as it sounds, He would have been returned to heaven but fallen short of His Father's intention for Him. And what of us? Had redemption's story failed, what benefit would Jesus have been to humanity either then or thousands of years later? Most believers would have pulled their swords, just like Peter did. Most, without discernment, without understanding would have fought against God's will, as horrible to the human soul as it was. It is this resistance to pain, suffering, trials that keeps the believer immature, impotent, and impossible to change.

Somehow, we don't think Jesus had a choice. We have come to believe that He absolutely had to give up His life. But He absolutely did not have to. That is what makes His sacrifice a love-driven, love-orchestrated, hope-compelled event. He voluntarily gave Himself to death that He might reign in life. The Father allowed the Son to hang on the Cross for six hours. The natural mind cannot understand it. Jesus had offered Himself. He suffered the agony of the whip, the crown of thorns, carrying the Cross. Then He was nailed to the Cross and it was dropped into the ground with a thud. It was done. Or was it? For six hours He suffered on that Cross. Why didn't Father take Him immediately? Why didn't Father let Him die as soon as the Cross was put into the ground? Why was it that six hours would have to pass before Jesus would cry out, "Father, why have You forsaken Me!?" Why did the entire day have to pass before Jesus could cry out, "It is finished" before He died? What was going on in the world of Spirit during these six hours? What was going on in the mind of our King as He hung there suffering during that time?

Consider this for a moment. Jesus had six hours to change His mind. He had six hours to determine that He'd had enough. Had the Father forsaken Him? Six hours of anguish, of hanging, slowly bleeding, slowly suffocating suggested that He had, indeed, been forsaken by His Father. For six hours, Jesus wrestled with excruciating pain; everything screamed, "God has forsaken you!"

Nonetheless, our King triumphed. At the end of the sixth hour, Jesus had erased all doubt, all uncertainty in His mind. In spite of the horrific and agonizing suffering, indescribable pain, with everything screaming to Him to give up, Jesus had determined His Father had, indeed, not forsaken Him and had, indeed prepared a place for Him at His Father's right hand. Our King had six hours to reconcile His destiny with the pain that wracked His body. During that time, He determined that He was, without question, redeeming mankind and proving His Father's love both to Himself and to humanity. The Cross was Jesus' final chance to say "No" to His Father.

No, there is nothing beautiful about the Cross. There is nothing that I love about it. It was the instrument of my Lord's execution. It was impossible to watch, dreadful to accept, mortifying to imagine. Jesus not only suffered for us but had every opportunity change His mind. That is the depth of His love. He hung on the Cross until every doubt, every thought of uncertainty was purged from His mind. For some, this is certainly an offensive train of thought. Suggesting for even a moment that Jesus needed anything that suffering could produce seems sacrilegious, but even the writer of the Book of Hebrews saw something most modern believers overlook.

> *In the days of His flesh, He offered up both prayers and supplications with loud crying and tears to the One able to save Him from death, and He was heard because of His piety. Although He was a Son, He learned obedience from the things which He suffered. And having been made perfect, He became to all those who obey Him the source of eternal salvation, being designated by God as a high priest according to the order of Melchizedek* (Hebrews 5:7-10 NASB).

A More Tolerable Faith

But we are taught a more tolerable Christianity. Modern Christianity teaches that all we have to do is believe God and everything should come to us. We always seem to conflate our salvation with our maturity as sons. Like the Ancients in the Wilderness, everything they needed to survive was provided. However, they did not experience the beginning of the next story until they crossed the River of their humanity, their fleshy struggle, the pain of discovering who they were. In Canaan, they began, by choice, to trust their King beyond how much they trusted themselves. When they crossed the River Jordan they "crossed" themselves. They took up their cross. They put their King before themselves. They started on the journey of maturing into the sons with whom He would rule. There, they finally began to understand, to experience and know their Father as their Father had already known them.

Sons on their way to maturity will resist blaming another for their struggles. They know that if "all things work together for good," then all things *do* work together for good. For it is clear, the more we trust our Father the less we will complain, whine, resist, and rebel. When we understand the magnitude of our Father's plan, His love and His absolute confidence, as well as our part in that plan, we will stand in stunned silence. We will have discovered how profoundly our Father has been at work within us and how profoundly we have fought against Him in the name of our religion. Our Father is still about the business of maturing sons for purposes yet to be revealed to an obstinate people still too dull of hearing to know what He is saying.

I AM a son. I do not want to miss God's purpose for me or any whom I love. I must learn to face the music, dance to the song the band plays, and grow up. Mature sons inherit everything. Immature sons, prodigal sons, demand their inheritance now and destroy the future for themselves, their children, and their children's children. Maybe that is why it is so difficult to pass this vibrant faith on to the next generation? Maybe we have settled for a lesser god? Maybe we are passing on a moral code, traditions that require only an outward adherence to list of commandments that have no power to actually, generationally change lives.

Modern Christianity

Let's face it. The story of the prodigal son is the story of modern Christianity. The prodigal had half a truth: He was a son. He was the son of a very wealthy father who loved him very deeply. He knew he had a share in a hefty inheritance. But he missed the other part of his birthright by a country mile. He understood well the part where he would receive enormous blessing. But alas, he could not (or would not) take the responsibility of his birthright. The part he understood was the part that had the power to make him temporarily rich. The part he did not understand was the part that would make him a king. It is sometimes hard to understand how he could grow up in the same environment as his brother and yet miss the point of transformation to a king. He certainly abdicated his right to rulership, having not grasped the importance of surrendered brokenness to his father.

Simply put, a person not trained in responsible discipline will not be able to rule over anything, even his own wealth, no matter how great it is. An even cursory glance to the entertainment, sports, and corporate world proves the point easily. Contrary to what many may believe, money does not mature; in fact, unless handling it is carefully taught, it only destroys. Forbes magazine reports that 70 percent of big lottery winners go bankrupt. A much larger group experience "winner's regret." One winner of $315 million laments that he ever won the money saying, "I wish I would have torn up the ticket." Unless the inner governance of the King is clearly established, any material blessing has the statistically proven end-doom.

I went into detail on this point in my book *The Forgotten Mountain*. Suffice it to say here that until the heart of the individual comes into union with God's heart, until surrendered repentance is a way of life, nothing else can be successfully ruled. For I, myself must be the first to come into alignment with my King before anything else will be cared for with frugality and faithfulness. Until "my mountain" is conquered and ruled by my King, I will not adequately conquer anything else, either spiritual or cultural.

Nonetheless, the prodigal went to his father demanding his share of what was rightfully his. The bold claims he made in his immature understanding of birthright broke his father's heart. But amazingly, he did what his son demanded. Having received all that was due him, the son was off to spend his money as carefree and recklessly as one would expect from a child. As we all know, at some point he ran out of money. It doesn't matter how long it took. But we know that when he found himself in a pigpen eating the clods that belonged to the hogs, he came to his senses. He experienced a transformation that only the difficulties of life could provoke. It is amazing how far we must fall in order to finally understand that we have missed the mark, failed the test, squandered what our Father had intended to be our lifelong security.

The boy wore the right clothes, said the right words, had the correct last name. He lived in his father's house, benefitted from the wealth of his father's greatness, understood what was his, and could not wait for the right time. He knew how beg, demand, decree, and declare in his father's name to grab his inheritance. Unfortunately, he missed the point that would make him the authentic son his father wanted him to become—a mature, functioning son whom dad could crown a king. Make no mistake. Just because the Bible says we are kings does not mean that we are automatically prepared to reign. Until we grow into that mighty burden of responsibility, we are like young Simba in the movie *The Lion King*, who just couldn't wait to be king. Although he was the heir apparent, he had to discover who he was and what was within him through the very real crucible of a life in the turbulence brought on by fear, rejection, and rebellion.

His coming to his senses was not a matter of keeping his name or his position as a son. It was a matter of going back to the beginning, as a hired hand, where he knew he would at least be kept alive. He already knew he had squandered his loot, but he did not want to lose his life as well.

If his change of heart was real, his future would be secure. Such is our Father's love for us. He did not command that his son be given a bunk with the hired hands. He commanded a feast fit for the return of a son who had been lost but now found.

Yes, there is no doubt we all want to be sons. So here is the good news—we are already sons. Even the prodigal knew who he was. He just missed the point of destiny that his position as son actually meant to him. But here is the bad news. Until we return to the Father's heart (not necessarily a church building), we will continue to miss our highest calling.

The Older Son

The difference between the prodigal and the mature son is always the process. Those who finagle a way around the process will always be dependent upon those who actually submit to the path of authentic maturity of soul and spirit. Even though the elder son stayed home, he still had issues of his own to deal with. There are some who like to point out that even the mature son didn't really know who he was. Of course he didn't. For he too was in process. But he was a "maturing son," not a "rebelling son."

The older son was in submission to his father, learning, discovering, walking into the destiny his father had determined. He had much to learn as well, but had determined that he was going to learn. He had made the decision that he would follow his father and not his own selfish ambitions or be sidetracked by the needs and passions of other men.

The son who stays under the tutelage of the father will not only inherit everything but he will grow into a loving, wise, prosperous, and competent person of broad influence in the earth. Such is our Elder

Brother, Jesus. He and His brethren will rule the world for generations with strength, compassion, love, and selflessness.

Sons Only Rule When the King Truly Rules the Sons

When the King rules the sons, they change the world with little effort, little fanfare, and require precious little gratuitous recognition. The passion of sons is quite simple. Our heart cry is the same as our brother, Paul:

> *I want to know Christ—yes, to know the power of his resurrection and participation in his sufferings, becoming like him in his death, and so, somehow, attaining to the resurrection from the dead* (Philippians 3:10-11 NIV).

Like Paul, my focused desire is that He might be seen clearly, correctly, and powerfully through the likes of a simple old man like me.

Thoughts for Sons in Process

1. Can you relate to the prodigal son in one way or another? Do you know what you must do?

2. Are you fully reconciled to your Father in your thoughts, words, and actions? How do you think your life would look different if you were?

3. Has the way of the Cross been made real in your life? Have you learned to embrace the Cross, which is the trials and difficulties of life? Are you taking the time to quiet your soul to learn from your sufferings?

Chapter 4

FATHER AND SON

My dear son,

  I know things don't always seem to go the way you want them to go. I know sometimes it makes you wonder where I AM, if you have ever heard My Voice. But when the storm is over, you always see more clearly, walk more securely, love more vibrantly. Take a step back for a minute and you will see that it is during these times that you experience the reality of our Father-son relationship more deeply. I AM always with you. I AM always gathering you. I AM always forgiving you, believing in you, always reassuring you that you are truly "becoming." By now I AM sure you have discovered that, unfortunately, it is only during difficult times that you run to Me, hold on to Me, need My love and tender reassurance that only a true Father can give you. That is OK; you are growing, becoming. Soon you will discover that you want to be in Me in the good times too. I AM at peace with your progress. You should be too. After all. I AM your Father and you are My son.

The Worst Day

  It was the worst experience in a long time. But then, it turned out to be the best experience. It was an awful day that turned into a triumphant day. My then-four-year-old son was in the backyard with the rest of us on a beautiful Saturday afternoon. We were working and playing, planting the garden and jumping into the small wading pool we had for our sons. Matthew was busy smelling the flowers planted along the side of the house when he was stung on his eye by a wasp. Of course, his screaming, crying, and running in circles was awful. When we finally caught up to him, he was frantic. The stinger was visible but was going deeper as the swelling got worse. Quickly, we decided that I would take him to the doctor while Cathy stayed with the other boys.

Now back in those days, there was no "urgent care" on every street corner. You simply called the doctor who met you at his office. It was a late Saturday afternoon, so there were no nurses and no assistants there. It was me, the doctor, and my screaming son. As he flailed about on the table we laid him on, it was clear the doctor could not work on him unless we could get him still. So our doctor wrapped Matt tightly in a blanket. He asked me to hold him down. The only part of Matt visible to me was the tear-filled swollen eye. As the doctor worked to remove the stinger, I looked into Matt's eye. It is amazing the message a young child can convey with just one eye. It was heartrending. "Daddy, what is happening? Why are you allowing this? Who is this guy and why is he hurting me? Help me! Make him stop! Why won't you stop him? Do you love me? I trusted you! You are supposed to keep me safe!" Wow, it still hurts to even write about it. Of course, what Matt didn't understand at his young age made him wonder if I really cared about him at all. But I wept as I saw him, heard his cries, and saw his tears. I tried to comfort him as I held him still so the doctor could, apparently, inflict even more pain on him. It was the worst day ever.

After what seemed to be an hour (but in reality was only two or three minutes), he was bandaged. I unwrapped him from the blanket. Then something remarkable happened. Here was a child whose father had seemly forced him to go through untold terror, who had seemed to aid a stranger in inflicting pain upon him. Nevertheless, this child leaped to his feet on the table and embraced me in almost hysterical crying. He squeezed my neck as hard as a four-year-old can squeeze.

At that moment, it turned into the best day ever. For at that moment, his spirit and mine were one. His heart and mine beat in synchronous harmony. In spiritual terms, his spirit bore witness with mine that he was my son; I was his dad, and I could be trusted no matter what it seemed like, and I would be with him through his worst pain.

But what would he have learned had he run from me? What would have been the end result of this awful situation had he not allowed himself to be loved by me while he suffered through it? Also, what if I would have simply responded in anger at his reaction to the pain? What if I would have been impatient with him, scolding him and refusing to comfort him? A child in pain is always looking for a parent's love, compassion, and comfort. A struggling child always needs tenderness, understanding, a soft touch, a gentle hug. It is in this interaction that a child learns the depth of his parent's love.

True Relationship

It was then that I began to discover what it truly meant to know that God was truly my Father. It was no longer a doctrine. It was no longer a simple Bible study or a song or a movement. It was a fact. I AM His son. For if I as a human, earthly dad can love with such intensity, how much more so my Father in heaven? If I allow my son to go through pain he cannot possibly understand yet is absolutely necessary, is it possible that my heavenly Father may sometimes have to do the same?

But more importantly, these times prove to me that I AM my Father's son. In the crucible of hard times, in the midst of the failure, confusion, and uncertainty of my human condition, I AM intended to discover what cannot be discovered any other way. When I embrace my

Father and He embraces me in comfort, reassurance, and love, I begin to see the depth of His commitment to me, His unwavering determined assurance that I AM His son. In spite of my wanderings and wonderings, in spite of my doubt and my rebellion, my hidden issues and my cover-ups, He continues to keep His hand upon me and lead me to my destiny. I AM His son. He gathers me and holds me even when I don't want to be held. He loves me even when I don't want to be loved. He forgives me even in the midst of my anger and pain. Yes, these are the moments that I learn the significance of my Father's love for me.

The antics of religion cannot make this any more real for me. In fact, religious attempts to make me feel what only authentic daily interaction with my Father can do for me will only frustrate me. I can jump through all the hoops required by man. I can pray all the right prayers and go to meetings ad infinitum. But they will only ensure that I live far short of the glory that is revealed in true sonship. I AM my Father's son. No man can tell me that. No song can cause the inner transformation that occurs when His Spirit embraces mine and His life intertwines with mine, convincing me, changing my mind, my perspective, and my reality from being alone in the universe to being one with my Father.

Most of our Bible studies, books, music, and schools teach us the anatomy of our Father but ignore the reality of the back-and-forth banter and fellowship of true relationship. The skeletal idea of a "father" means little to me and offers no insight as to His personality, love, compassion, desires, or the intentions of His heart. There is no doubt as to why so many feel empty after an exhaustive Bible class. We learn so much about God but never come to experientially know Him any better than we did beforehand. How can we tout a "family atmosphere" among believers when most of what we know of our Father is limited to what another person tells us about Him?

Jesus spoke directly and without compromise about this when He rebuked the religious leaders with these words: "You search the Scriptures because, in them, you think you have eternal life. But all the Scriptures point to Me" (see John 5:39). Of course, there is a lot more to eternal life than going to heaven. If all God did for us was to buy us a ticket to heaven, then books like the one you are now holding in your hands would be useless indeed. In that case, we would need to know only how to get that elusive ticket and how to hold on to it until we need it at the gates of heaven. But when salvation was accomplished at His resurrection, man received the power to become mature sons—sons who have the power to rule wherever they are and according to the nature and the Spirit of their Father.

Jesus taught us to pray, "Thy Kingdom come, Thy will be done in earth, as it is in heaven" (Matt. 6:10 KJV). Our Father's intention was not merely for man to go to heaven. Rather, He always intended heaven to come to earth through the life and power of maturing sons who have learned obedience through the things they suffer, as did our Elder Brother as He walked the earth. Thus, through the lives of maturing sons heaven would certainly be seen and felt upon this planet as His Kingdom is established in the hearts of sons everywhere.

Still Thirsty

In the last day, that great day of the feast, Jesus stood and cried, saying, If any man thirst, let him come unto me, and drink (John 7:37 KJV).

The Feast of Tabernacles was an awesome and celebratory time for the Jews. It was a seven-day feast to fill the stomach and fill the soul. It was a day and night celebration that had been kept by the nation of Israel for three thousand years. Jesus went up to Jerusalem on the seventh day, which was, by all accounts, the greatest day of the feast.

His comment that day was far more than just a call to those who were not satisfied. After seven days of what should have been the most fulfilling time of the year, the spirit, soul, and body of those who attended the feast should have been overwhelmingly satisfied. But it was on that day that Jesus stepped in their party with a most compelling indictment when He cried out, "Is anyone thirsty?"

The question must have shaken them to the core. After a week of religious activity, after a week of learning about God, learning the rules of the religion, listening to teachers expounding on the Torah, was there anyone still unsatisfied? Was there anyone still craving for more than all the hype of religious fanfare? The point is quite simple. The "things of God" do not satisfy for very long, just as an ice cream cone doesn't satisfy in place of a meal. A letter does not satisfy as a voice satisfies. A photograph does not satisfy as much as seeing that person face to face. A description of a person holds no advantage over a touch from them. The reality of authentic friendship cannot be duplicated with the same degree of satisfaction any other way. Our Father has always wanted sons with whom He would interact, converse, and work together to do His will in the earth.

Words like *intimacy* are often overused in trying to describe a relationship that does not actually exist between most believers and their heavenly Father. We use human words of physical endearment like "kiss," "the warmth of His embrace," "the beat of His heart," etc. Yet, too many times, these are only elusive and hopeful descriptions of those who have not actually experienced His Fatherhood in the reality of spiritual union. I am speaking of union where your spirit is literally becoming one with His—where His Life rests within you. Such feelings are mostly beyond human ability to adequately express to any level of accuracy. Using human terms of endearment is, at best, a poor substitute for the authentic spiritual union that God intends between Him and His sons.

The Glory, the Father, and You

Ought not Christ to have suffered these things, and to enter into his glory? (Luke 24:26 KJV)

For I reckon that the sufferings of this present time are not worthy to be compared with the glory which shall be revealed in us (Romans 8:18 KJV).

It is to the glory of God that His sons can lovingly embrace their Father in hard times. For glory is not an external presence, an external feeling, or an external expression of the Divine. It is an internal reality of substantive, experiential reality that empowers the inner man to great exploits, great accomplishments, great expressions of His love to the world, whether that world is the home, the community, a nation, or the entire earth. The greatness of what we do is not measured in volume; it is measured in effectiveness in the work within arm's reach. The trials of life should turn us inward to find His Life so that we may then turn outward with the strength to do what may seem to be the impossible.

Life's trying times should bring us to a place of absolute surrender to Him. He expects them to drive us to the source of Divine Everything within. But contemporary believers are often too stuck on the external. We are too easily satisfied to be wowed by the smoke and fire of the temporal, the things that tantalize the outer man, therefore making the inner discovery unnecessary. But the glory that is eternal is not detected by the naked eye. It is the inner glory, that churning, life-changing interaction with the Christ of God that makes the weak strong, the timid powerful, the lonely fulfilled, the rejected of man into a maturing son of God. The best thing that can happen for a believer is for God to shut off the external crutches that feed the five senses so that the believer will search within his own heart to find the King resting comfortably in his heart. This is where real peace is found and authentic rest is established.

Real Glory

Glory is the one term with otherworldly implications that should not be dumbed down to appease the ones who have no clue, no desire, and no intention of ever surrendering. His eternal glory should never be compromised in order to make it easier on those who do not or will not pay the dues of surrender to develop the eyesight of authentic spiritual vision. The inner reality of God is meant to be a moment-by-moment experience. It is not withheld from some as many have argued. However, it is restricted—not by God but by those who will not give of themselves that they might see Him as He truly is. Those who are willing to surrender to the process of maturity will, without question, experience Him just as the Ancients did when they obediently crossed the Jordan.

Glory is a word that sets the heart ablaze with hunger for more than has yet been experienced. Glory is the reality that turns faith into substance and hope into experience. Glory is the by-product of obedience and abides within us forever. It does not come and go like the manna in the Wilderness. Our Father comes to permanently restore His manifest Life to His sons. His glory is the King Himself who abides permanently within us.

> *And the glory which thou gavest me I have given them; that they may be one, even as we are one* (John 17:22 KJV).

Those who have not experienced this will argue all day long, but their arguments have no substance as they have only doctrine to defend their position that Glory comes and goes. The "Glory" on the Mercy Seat is there to stay. Because our hearts are the true Mercy Seat, "Glory" is there to stay as well. "Glory" is, in fact, the essence, the substance, the very reality of our Father. Once you have tasted this incredible union, you will not ever be satisfied with anything less.

If I'd Only Known

Unfortunately we do not have the option of going back to redo life. But if we are attentive, we will find that God is putting all kinds of powerful lessons before us today that can serve us well in the future—if we are soft and teachable. When my son jumped into my arms after the doctor removed that mean old stinger, I wept at the power of love. I was in awe of the strength of conviction in such a young child that would enable him to maintain his unwavering trust in me, even after I apparently caused more pain for him.

My dear son, Matt! What a lesson you taught me! What a living example of unconditional trust in someone whom he believed had unconditional love for him, even when he didn't understand! May God help us to run to Him as Matt jumped into my arms on that hot Saturday evening so many years ago. On that spontaneous yet powerful moment, time stood still. In that moment, his spirit was glued to mine and he knew, without a doubt, that he was my son and I was his daddy. For that moment, all was right with the world.

My Father's Dream

I have no desire to follow a good code of ethics or specified moral standards as the primary rule of my life. It is my union with my Father that transforms me into a person who is loving and honorable, moral and trustworthy, ethical and true. My union with Him makes me into someone who can live the dream that my Father has dreamed for me. To that end, it is my desire to please Him in all I do and all I AM. That passion compels me to surrender every day so that nothing can hinder the visibility of my Lord through me. I want to know Him in the power of His resurrection, the fellowship of His suffering while being willing to die to the daily complications of mortal flesh that try to keep me at arm's length from my Father.

My daily prayer echoes the words of one of the Ancients, the Apostle Paul.

> *I count everything as loss compared to the possession of the priceless privilege (the overwhelming preciousness, the surpassing worth, and supreme advantage) of knowing Christ Jesus my Lord and of progressively becoming more deeply and intimately acquainted with Him [of perceiving and recognizing and understanding Him more fully and clearly]. For His sake I have lost everything and consider it all to be mere rubbish (refuse, dregs), in order that I may win (gain) Christ (the Anointed One), and that I may [actually] be found and known as in Him, not having any [self-achieved] righteousness that can be called my own, based on my obedience to the Law's demands (ritualistic uprightness and supposed right standing with God thus acquired), but possessing that [genuine righteousness] which comes through faith in Christ (the Anointed One), the [truly] right standing with God, which comes from God by [saving] faith.*
>
> *[For my determined purpose is] that I may know Him [that I may progressively become more deeply and intimately acquainted with Him, perceiving and recognizing and understanding the wonders of His Person more strongly and more clearly], and that I may in that same way come to know the power outflowing from His resurrection [which it exerts over believers], and that I may so*

share His sufferings as to be continually transformed [in spirit into His likeness even] to His death, [in the hope] that if possible I may attain to the [spiritual and moral] resurrection [that lifts me] out from among the dead [even while in the body] (Philippians 3:8-11 AMPC).

Even so, may it be according to these words.

Meditations for a Determined Son

1. Can you relate to Matt's experience with his father? When have you had a similar moment with your heavenly Father?

2. Can you see the powerful love experience of trustingly turning to Him in our pain and loving Him in spite of what we don't understand?

3. Have you "seen" the glory within you that is invisible to the naked eye?

Chapter 5

NO OTHER WAY

My dear son,

If you could only see how focused your Father is on your well-being, your purpose. I have it on good intel that He is determined to see you fulfill your life's calling. To that end, stop trying to please, impress, or convince mere man who you are. Rather, look to your Father, Who minute by minute is trying to get your attention. But you **must** understand this—He is **not** in the box you expect Him to be in; but then, neither is your destiny. Be courageous! Lay aside your stubborn heart and listen for what you do not expect to hear. He is talking loud and clear. And He has lots to say. Hush! Don't argue with me. God's talking—to you.

In our endeavor to find Him in all His blessing, we tend to take the path that appears to be the quickest way to getting all that is coming to us and the fulfillment of our Father's dream for us. But as we saw with the prodigal son, there are no shortcuts that lead to permanent growth.

And without genuine growth, there is no authentic maturity. The growth process requires daily obedience, daily dying to self-promotion, self-exaltation, self-gratification, and self-centered lifestyles. These only hinder the maturation process and prolong a life of confusion, defeat, and uncertainty. Of course, it would be far easier to simply "believe" our way to success, "worship" our way to maturity, "fast" our way to the dream God has dreamed for us. But there is no simple road to maturity. This path requires more patience than we would ever want to admit.

Our culture has conditioned us to expect instant gratification in every area of life. The Christian Charismatic world also teaches that simple confession of faith magically gives us everything that the Bible promises. Of course, that did not work out so well for the prodigal and it does not work out either for those who have not understood the time it takes to grow into a mature son. Even Jesus "learned obedience through the things He suffered." It will be no different for us. Nonetheless, the popular narrative on receiving our Father's promises simply because we deserve them or because He purchased them for us on the Cross is quite contrary to what the Scriptures actually teach. Their fulfillment is activated by our personal surrender.

Students who slide through school doing as little work as possible will fail in their chosen professions if they cannot do what is indicated by their degree of training. Even receiving a diploma does not guarantee success. The real test of what our diploma says you can do is proven in the ability to get the job done. In the business world, few can afford to hire someone who does not have the skills that are required for the job.

When I was actively managing Destiny Image, I would often have friends ask me to hire their child or someone they knew. Of course, my initial response was, "Sure, have them come and fill out an application for whatever job they are interested in. We will give them an evaluation to see their proficiency." For some, that was not exactly what they had in mind. They thought that our friendship was enough for me to hire their recommended prospect with or without the ability needed. Others would simply say that the test was not necessary because they already knew how to do the work. In both cases, someone was expecting me to pay the price for someone who never did or never wanted to pay the price for training, competency, and testing. The key to successfully getting a job and progressing in a profession should be obvious: Work hard to learn all the necessary skills to be an asset to the company. Any other attitude is exactly what is wrong with much of the government and the religious system. An attitude of entitlement has permeated both sectors and is the downfall of both. People fail when they take a shortcut, thinking that the shortcut will bring them the same success as they would enjoy if they had done all the work. In the real world, it does not work that way.

When my twin brother and I were kids, my dad would send us out into the woods after school to find firewood for the old furnace that heated our home. In the beginning, Ron and I thought we knew how to make our work easier by creating the appearance that we had done what he wanted. We would take the wheelbarrow out to the wooded acres behind our house and would lay the wood in such a manner that it appeared that the wheelbarrow was full of wood when, in reality, we only had a few pieces across the top. We were so smart, or so we thought! We did what dad wanted us to do—and only in a fraction of the time. But on those nights, the whole family ended up being cold. We learned quickly that there were no shortcuts to a warm house. We had to actually bring in a full load of wood if we were to stay warm.

The difference between the prodigal and the mature son is always the process. Those who finagle a way around the process will always be dependent upon those who actually submit to the path of authentic maturity of soul and spirit. A lifetime of finagling creates a lifestyle of frustration, uncertainty, and aimlessness, whereas engaging with the maturing process of our King brings not only maturity but purposeful fulfillment in everyday life.

From Little Children to Young Men to Fathers (From Glory to Glory)

No one benefits from immaturity. No one achieves their goals, lives their dreams, or experiences unshakable peace by being protective of their weaknesses, their fleshy antics, or childish rants. The culture, the society, the Church that Jesus is building is dependent on the growth of the individuals within it. Of course, we are a Body; we are members of one another. Of course, we gain strength from one another. But knowing all this in theory is not enough. It must become the primary functionality of everyday life. We are not "one" just because the Bible says we are. We do not automatically sit in heavenly places. Our elder Brother provided the Way for these things to become a daily lifestyle and experience. But we must submit to that Way. We must, individually, allow the work of our Father to have its full effect in our hearts, minds, and our lives. To be seated in heavenly places is the destiny, but submitting to the discipline of the King is the process that activates that reality in our lives.

No, maturity will not happen instantaneously any more than entering the Promised Land for the children of Israel meant that they would suddenly experience the end of their struggle and pain. Their decision to enter the Promised Land only meant they had decided to believe God. It meant that their obedience would overcome their fear, for it is only when we decide to obey God in spite of our fears that we begin to grow in maturity.

You see, it was the Ancients' *obedience* that finally parted the Jordan River, giving them the opportunity take the land that the Father had promised to them. Their decision to cross was just the beginning of the next part of their journey. Certainly, it was the sacrifice of the Lamb that freed them from the bondage and slavery of Egypt, but it would be their own sacrifice that would bring them into the fullness of God's plan for them. The Jordan marked a new day of trusting in Him and responding to His leading, even when that direction brought them directly into the path of the enemy.

When the Ancients made the decision to cross the River, the death to themselves was as real as the death of the lambs when they left Egypt. For this death would separate them forever from the inner fleshy passions that kept them far short of God's glory. This death may not have been physical, but it was certainly death nonetheless. They had to die to their wanton lusts, their secret sins, their hate, anger, and rebellious hearts. They would have to change their hearts and focus their future on their allegiance to their Father. They would have to stop "hiding" those things that were rampant within them. They would have to decrease as the very reign of the King increased within them. They would have to deny the hidden and deadly things that they loved. They would have to make the conscious decision to expose and confess all that separated them, distracted them, and ultimately denied them from the very thing they wanted most—union with God. This was to be the journey for the Ancients, and it is the same journey for each one of us today.

The giants in the land were as real as they come. The seeming certainty of death followed them wherever their feet stepped in the Promised Land. Yes, it was their land, but it was occupied territory.

The Ancients would have to face each enemy and defeat them just as we have to face the enemies of our soul and defeat them. This requires focused concentration, attentive determination, and purposeful resolve to let God bring authentic transformation within our hearts. But the enemies of our soul find harbor in our minds when we allow rampant, unharnessed, unrepented thoughts to distract us from our inheritance.

Our Father wants us to live in purity, destiny, and lavished love, but we will never experience the union we desire as long as we ignore the things that separate us from Him. Remember, the Promised Land is flowing with milk and honey, but it still must be conquered before we can enjoy its produce. No wonder the Father commands us to "sit at My right hand until I make your enemies a footstool for your feet" (see Luke 20:42-43). Being seated with the Father is not the end of the war; it is the beginning of it.

Somewhere along the road, we were sold a bill of goods that has little resemblance to the truth. Many of us have come to believe that the Promised Land is heaven. The problem is that the Promised Land was still full of enemies, giants, things that go "bump" in the night! None of that junk is in heaven. The Promised Land and the Most Holy Place are synchronous to our hearts. We are the dwelling place of God. Just as the Ancients did, we also must surrender the land of our hearts that He might truly reign there in all His majesty and glory.

The Weapons of Our Warfare

One does not defeat the enemy by ignoring him, shouting Scripture at him, rebuking him, or "covering ourselves with the Blood of the Lamb." These are not magic phrases that we can use on a whim. The enemy is put under our feet by careful, methodical obedience, repentance, and change. When the heart is right and your King has specifically instructed in a particular situation, these may work. But remember, they only work because He is leading. If we use these methods and nothing happens, there is something missing and we must find what's missing rather than continuously going down a fruitless path. The enemy of our soul is defeated by denying him access to our thoughts and desires, not by using Scripture like magic, pretending he isn't there, or hiding under a pillar of smoke or fire.

As we grow in Him, it becomes easier to make a stand. When we do, the enemy runs like the defeated enemy he truly is. When our life is clothed with our Father's life through sacrifice and obedience, we are already covered, hidden in Him. When we stand firm, not allowing him to feed on our secret cravings, not allowing him to lie to us, belittle us, or deny our Father's love to us, we are making a statement that shines like a beacon in the spirit realm that we are one not to be trifled with.

Unfortunately, failure seems to come all too frequently. The things we want to do we find ourselves not doing. The very things we hate seem to lurk around every corner. But thank God for His mercy. Even when we must repent often, sometimes very often, for the same thing, He is there to quickly forgive and gather us. This will actually keep us humble, reminding us of who and what we are apart from His gracious love. When I find myself in need of repentance, I've learned to do it quickly so as not to give myself time to blame someone else or convince myself it wasn't a sin after all. Blame shifting is what got us all in trouble in the Garden, and we must still carefully guard against it.

A Son by God's Design

You have been made a son in body, soul, and spirit. God help the one who tries to take that away from you. As I have said before, you are a son whether you are a prodigal or a maturing son. The sooner you see this in your heart, the sooner you will begin to trust your Father in a whole new light and learn to listen more carefully to His words to you. As long as you respond to your Father within, you will be able to overcome the enemies without. Learning a lifestyle of inner surrender to His governance causes His Life to flood your thoughts and your spirit. You begin to yield to the truth that *is* your Father and you begin to grow in the knowledge of Him. The peace that passes all understanding does not come from a doctrine. Peace is a reality born in your heart through the crucible of unfortunate events to which you respond with faith, eternal reassurance, and Divine expectation.

Do not make the mistake of thinking I am renouncing doctrine. Far be it from that. But doctrine without experience is like learning to fly on a simulator without ever going into the sky behind the pilot's seat. The difference between merely knowing a good teaching in our head and having the experience in our heart and life is staggering. You are a son. That fact, in itself, will not send the enemy running. You must know who you are *by experience* instead of just doctrine. From the moment a person comes to Jesus, their sonship is the first thing that should be taught. For it is not merely believing the doctrines of repentance, sanctification, or sonship that sets us free, but the practice of them. It is through practice that we experience His presence every day. It is the *doing* of His word that makes us free.

> *Whoever comes to Me, and hears My sayings and does them, I will show you whom he is like: He is like a man building a house, who dug deep and laid the foundation on the rock. And when the flood arose, the stream beat vehemently against that house, and could not shake it, for it was founded on the rock* (Luke 6:47-48).

Success in God's Eyes

But what does this really all mean in the practical sense? How does this affect my life on this planet in the real world? Cathy and I raised sons. One is a successful IT guru. One is the CEO of Destiny Image. Another is a successful attorney and CEO of *It's Supernatural*. One has a small business in Arizona, and another is a contractor. These professions are as different as they can be. Each has its unique requirements of knowledge and expertise. But collectively, our sons have one thing in common—they were raised, equipped, and trained by the same father and mother. Their foundational maturity was planted deep in their hearts over the course of their upbringing. Therefore, whatever they choose to do in life, they will succeed because they were instructed and disciplined in the ways of success. Those who are raised in this fashion learn to fear nothing. Obstacles are simply temporary inconveniences. Their challenges are met head-on and overcome in due time. Their achievements in life will be talked about for a long time, but the root of their achievements lies hidden within them. Their greatest achievements are simply that they learned to yield to the process, allowed themselves to be taught, and were not controlled by arrogance or selfish ambition. The evidence of their daily process is in their accomplishments, and all who are around them benefit. They are, first and foremost, sons.

The evidence of what turns us from a mere human into a maturing son is never what is visible by the world's standards. The authentic evidence will always be the attributes of the King that are visible through our lives. The permanent transformations that we experience in this life serve us for eternity. Therefore, there must be far more importance to this life than we have understood when we take into account the eternity we are all going to experience. The inner structure of His rule and reign that is established within us, here in the crucible of this dimension, shall be to the glory of our King forever.

I have been in business for more than 30 years. I have pastored, counseled, and spoken in more settings than I can remember. There are a few things of which I am certain after all these years in His service— the best folks are rarely at the top. The most giving, the most loving, compassionate, caring people I have met are primarily the hidden ones. They are the ones who have struggled more than most. Their success has been limited, their laurels infrequent, and their résumé barren. But they have faithfully served and sacrificed in ways that no one saw, loved when others turned aside, and gave when no one was watching. These folks are known by few. Nevertheless, they will reign with Him while many of the "powerful ones" will be relegated to a lower place. "But many who are first will be last, and the last first" (Mark 10:31).

This uncanny Divine focus on the heart, the inner life, should give us all pause. For He sees what no others see. In the quietness of our private life, choosing to live for Him even with no one around to see us prepares us for a destiny that goes far beyond time and space. At our last breath, our hearts will be glad that we have been faithful to Him without anyone watching. We will rejoice that we have loved Him with no hidden agenda and have served Him with only the knowledge of pleasing Him as our reward. We will find our fulfillment in this—that we have been to Him the obedient son, that we have been to Him all He asked of us. Yes, the Blood of the Lamb gets us to heaven, but it is the covenantal, sacrificial life of the believer that is our eternal offering to our Father, to Whom we have pledged our loyalty, given our life, and borne witness to in the world.

How Does This Work in the Real World?

> *For the earnest expectation of the creation eagerly waits for the revealing of the sons of God. For the creation was subjected to futility, not willingly, but because of Him who subjected it in hope; because the creation itself also will be delivered from the bondage of corruption into the glorious liberty of the children of God. For we know that the whole creation groans and labors with birth pangs together until now* (Romans 8:19-22).

For too many years, the things we have believed have been relegated to church and Sunday school. There has been precious little real-world evidence that anything we believe actually works outside the confines of the religious system—even the denominational Charismatic, Pentecostal systems of belief. Of course, this is exactly why Christianity has become the laughingstock of most of the world. We have touted a faith with moral standards, supernatural power, and transformational reality, but we have delivered a weak, politically motivated orthodoxy with no hint of functional reality, a substandard display of religious life with no inner moral compass. The world craves real hope, real answers. They have looked to us for the living God we say we have, but instead we have more often than not delivered a dead religion with no authentic love and compassion. The world needs sons. The Church Jesus is building needs sons. A demonstrable reality that actually *is* what it claims it is will send shockwaves over the earth in the form of a love that is otherworldly and Divine. The manifestation of our sonship will release the compassionate deeds of a gathering God into a world that is desperate for proof that He cares for mankind's well-being.

Maturing sons are always ready to pay the ultimate price to be the convincing splendor of God in the earth. Of us, He says, "Gather My godly ones to Me, those who have made a covenant with Me by sacrifice" (Ps. 50:5 AMP). This desire to gather us to Himself is the groan of the Father through the ages. His sons are in tune with the cry of His heart, for they also feel His very groan within them. Those who cut covenant by sacrifice can be trusted, for they have paid the price of obedience. They will honestly, purely, faithfully be the lamp through which the Light of the World will be seen. The Ancients declared that Word had to become flesh. The Word still needs to become flesh in us, His sons. Maturing sons, bearing the image of the Christ of God, are the irrefutable proof that all things Divine can be expressed in time and space just as He has promised. The likes of you and I living a surrendered life so that He can be seen, experienced, showcased in this dimension is the result of the sacrificial covenant with our Father.

The successful, functional reality of understanding our place as a son cannot be overstated. Those who have been willing to pay the price will reign in this life and the next. These will yield to God's destiny whether that destiny sends them to the nations or keeps them in a single profession for a lifetime, raising children in the fear and admonition of the Lord. Whatever He calls them to, they will be the lamp in that place for the Son of God to shine through. It is His intention to showcase His irresistible love and overcoming power through His obedient, surrendered sons so that His glory will be seen over the entire earth.

Questions for the Courageous

1. What does true success look like in your life? If you don't see it, are you prepared to take the steps necessary to step into your destiny?

2. Can you list some of the attributes of your King that you see in your life at this moment?

3. Are there attributes of the King that still escape you but you want to see developed in your life? What are they?

4. Do you quiet your life that you might hear His Voice when He teaches you, encourages you, convicts you of sin, and leads you into the new? Do you have a regular habit of listening to Him, or is it something less?

Chapter 6

TWO SACRIFICES

> My dear son,
> The day is coming when the full extent of what it means to be My son will be clear to you. My son, the day is coming when the hard reality of coming to maturity will dawn on you. In that moment, you will know the difference between what is coming to you as My son and what your responsibility is as My son. If you get the first but don't hang around for the second, the glory you want, the union you see, will be out of your reach. Do not settle for the things that tantalize the natural man. For what you see is the lesser of your position as My son. There is more to you than meets the eye. If you stay focused, stay close, stay surrendered, there is no end to who you can become. There is no doubt that Who you inherit will be far more eternal that what you inherit.

Leaving Egypt

When Israel left Egypt, God made a promise to them that initiated the Passover sacrifices. "But Moses said to the people, 'Do not fear! Stand by and see the salvation of the Lord which He will accomplish for you today; for the Egyptians whom you have seen today, you will never see them again forever'" (Exod. 14:13 NASB). And they never did. The Egyptians would no longer be a threat to them for they would never see them again. Their Father had made it clear that their deliverance was once and for all. Egypt would be a thing of the past. A whole new life was now beginning as they turned their backs on their former slave masters.

The physical threat of the Egyptian army came to an end as God had declared. But it would take *leaving* the Wilderness for Israel to understand that the "Egyptians" (the fears that remained lodged in their minds) were truly defeated. The Wilderness mindset of uncertainty and fear of their future kept them wandering, looking over their shoulder, and falling far short of Father God's ultimate intention for them. Israel would have to grow up, to mature as a people. They would have to mentally move on from being sons under the domination of evil slave masters to sons who would be ready to face their giants and find victory in their own land. They would have to mature from the whining uncertainty of Wilderness existence to the glorious manifestation of the mature sons of God. Only then would they actually witness the powerful, loving intent of their Father. And only then would the rest of the world be able to not only witness but also experience their Father's love as well.

In order for the children of Israel to be delivered from Egypt, sacrificial blood had to be shed. The Passover Lamb ensured that Israel would be protected as they fled the bondage of their Egyptian slave masters. This is, of course, a picture of the Lamb of God, whose sacrificial death on the Cross secured deliverance from the slave masters of sin and death. Israel fled into the Wilderness with the Egyptian army in hot pursuit, but the promise of God held true and no one was lost in their flight from Pharaoh. This is a principle for us also: When any man trusts the Lamb of God, we too escape our bondage into the relative safety of the Wilderness.

It didn't take much faith for the children of Israel to flee Egypt. The Scriptures do not record resistance or doubt among the people. They were more than ready to flee Egyptian bondage. They were looking for a Deliverer. But it was not their faith that delivered them. They hated their life and would have done anything to get free of it. It was actually the determined love of their Father that opened the way of escape. They fled because God had independently determined that these were His people and He would deliver them.

And who would otherwise want to stay in the tyranny of slavery, suffering, uncertainty, and most certainly an early death? No, Israel was ready to take advantage of the sacrificial Lamb as instructed by Moses. They were done with cutting straw, hauling water, and making bricks. They were done living at the end of the slave masters' whips. When Moses announced it was time to go, they packed their bags and waited for word to get out of town. But as Israel soon discovered, they were on a journey with a destination that was far more powerful than merely leaving Egyptian bondage.

Leaving the Wilderness

It was Father God's focused love and resolute plan that miraculously delivered Israel that fateful day in ancient Egypt. But now that they were in the Wilderness, how would they ever get to the Promised Land? Before them lay the daunting task of moving a million people with all their possessions and herds across a Wilderness they had never seen, being led by a man they did not know who said he heard from a God they had never seen and upon whom they had already waited hundreds of years for their freedom. How would Israel ever reach this so-called "Promised Land"? How would they ever step into the full promise of God, a land of their own, a land flowing with milk and honey?

It wasn't enough that the Wilderness was fraught with dangers and uncertainties. Israel had also brought with them their temptations, fears, doubts, and stubbornness. They were free from the immediate threat, but a much deeper threat overshadowed them—a threat that would take them 40 years to overcome. Nonetheless, their Father was gracious to a fault. He took care of them in every detail. He was with them. Their lives were surrounded with the miraculous activity of God day and night. Their clothes never wore out and grew as they grew. Their shoes never wore out. They experienced the daily, visible miracles of a pillar of smoke to keep them cool in the sweltering heat of the desert sun. At night, they were all warmed by a pillar of fire. A Rock followed their wanderings with a river of water flowing from it that was plentiful enough to supply the needs of all the people plus all their livestock. By any measure, it was a mighty flowing river. Their Father fed them with manna from heaven and quail that simply fell from the sky. He appeared to Moses on a regular basis in ways that the entire camp could witness. The sacrificial Lamb that delivered them from Egypt was behind them. The Wilderness was before them. Their Father's focus for them was directly forward to Canaan. They had all they needed to step into the destiny of their heavenly Father who had, without doubt, provided for them at every turn.

The continuous miracles that kept them alive in the Wilderness were not a result of their faith, for they had none. They lived in fear, rebellion, debauchery, confusion and doubt. They fought one another, resisted God, and fulfilled every lust of their fleshy existence. Nonetheless, God cared for them as their loving Father. Their faith was not the determining factor of their safety and sustenance. It was their Father who kept them. He delivered them by His mighty hand and kept them with equal intensity until they reached the Jordan River. It would be a long road to maturity from the rebellious sons in Egypt to the obedient sons who would step into their destiny as they crossed into Canaan.

No Power to Cross the River

After over 40 years of wandering, they realized that all the miracles they experienced and all the power displayed in their lives was not enough to part the Jordan River for them. The truth is the miraculous power of the Wilderness was never intended to have the capability to bring them over. That was not the purpose of the signs and wonders. The supernatural display in the Wilderness was only meant to keep them alive in their rebellion and unbelief. The fact is, if anything, they were unwilling to let go of those miracles. They could not imagine life without the provision of this "Wilderness God" whom they did not yet know as their Father.

Life in the Wilderness was much easier. Much easier, that is, on the fleshy side of man—that very human, rebellious, opinionated part of us that does all it can to secure a place far from accountability before God. Considering that Canaan was overrun by their enemies, the Wilderness was a relative oasis! It is true that as long as Israel refused to engage the giants they remained in the Wilderness, but they doomed themselves to live miserably short of the glory intended for them. Ironically, the Wilderness miracles, the sustaining signs and wonders of their wandering years became a stumbling block that kept them from their destiny.

This is a very interesting thought: They could not physically enter the Promised Land until they were emotionally ready to face the daunting challenge to change. He loved them too deeply to allow them to step into their inheritance without the willingness to develop the strength of character necessary to properly administrate it. Yet, even crossing the Jordan was not the end of the journey. It was not the goal of their existence. Rather, it was the beginning of a new way of life. It was the beginning of the methodical destruction of the enemies of their souls. The decision they made to cross the River meant they would have to face their giants, those things that seemed too strong, too persistent, and too entrenched to be removed from their land.

Where Is the Power?

To cross the River, they would need to find the source of the power that would be required for them to truly have the new beginning. The power that would part the Jordan was nowhere in the Wilderness. Search as they might, wander as they might from one end of that Wilderness to the other, they would never find the power to cross the River, for the power that would usher in a new dispensation of union was found in an unlikely place indeed. It was found within them. Their obedience released a power never before experienced by mere mortals. Their obedience to their Father was proof that they had finally tired of their own ways while wandering in the Wilderness. It said they were ready to do it God's way, even if it meant death.

There is no doubt that contemporary believers need also to look within for the strength they need to begin their new adventure into the unknown of union with God. It is only this power within that will have the overcoming ability to scatter the enemies that plague our souls. For those who will not be content with the mundane, this is the answer that has eluded them. The delivering power of the Christ of God awaits and is always available to the obedient.

But make no mistake, obedience *does* mean death! Just as the sacrifice of the Lamb freed the Ancients from the bondage they hated in Egypt, so they, themselves, would become the sacrifice that would deliver them from the Wilderness they had become accustomed to. They had previously fled the outer bondage they hated in Egypt, but now they would have to flee a different sort of bondage—the hidden, wanton cravings of their soul. At the banks of the Jordan they would need to determine who they would follow. The choice could not be more clear—would they follow the sustaining but directionless miracles of Wilderness life, or would they obey their Father who would once and for all give them the opportunity to experience wholeness without deterioration, union without regret, and destiny without distraction?

While still in the Wilderness, there was no opportunity to grow in relationship with their Father, no chance to surrender to authentic change. To continue their journey to mature sons, they would have to first trust Him to protect them in the process of transformation. Fueled by frustration with their aimless way of life, some would come to a decision that would ensure their future in the plan of God. They did not have to die a meaningless death in the Wilderness, short of His glory and far from their destiny. In Canaan, they would find their God in a new way. He was not only their God, their Healer, and their Deliverer, but He was also their Father. For here, they would learn His ways. Here they would see Him fight their battles, give them peace, and know Him as the faithful Father that He is.

Finally, here they would begin to understand that the Rock out of which flowed that mighty river would still be with them. Now, however, it would be within them. But this time it would not be literal water; rather, it would be the very life force of the King Himself covering the whole world like the waters cover the sea. The bread that fell from heaven would be the Bread of Life, once again, the Christ of God, Who would nourish them and feed all those who came to Him. The pillars of smoke and fire would be the sustaining miracles that would give them inner strength, making them a shelter from the storms of life. No, the Wilderness miracles would not disappear. Rather, they would find a new home in the hearts of those who would be obedient to their Father.

The key was their simple obedience and the result was the parting of the Jordan River.

Leaving the Wilderness

Once Israel crossed the Jordan River, they never again longed to go back to Egypt. The querulous arguments about returning to slavery were gone. Their focus had become singular in intent and purpose. And why not? There were giants in the land! The battles ahead of them were real and they were to the death. Israel's focus was acquiring dominion in the land their Father had given them. They understood that governance of the land would be impossible while their enemies still occupied the territory belonging to them. They knew that they would have to engage the enemy as their Father directed them in order to be victorious. They had made the decision to die before they crossed the River. Now, the battle would rage. Israel, like their Father, would not be trifled with.

But something must have snapped in them when the last of those who actually fled Egypt fell in the Wilderness. There was finally nothing holding them back, no one to plant fear in their hearts, no one to resist the intention of their heart to obey their Father and ours. For the first time in their lives, they were free to follow their hearts. It is, indeed, an awesome sense of liberty when one determines to follow their heart's desire instead of being controlled, limited, and intimidated by those who live in fear. This is a critical lesson to take to heart, even today. The victorious are those who follow the King, not those who cower in unbelief and fear.

Our Quantum Leap

A quantum leap is an abrupt transition—a huge step forward into the new, the unexplored. It is a movement from the much lesser to the much greater. When Paul said that "He [Jesus] rescued us from the domain of darkness, and transferred us to the kingdom of His beloved Son" (Col. 1:13 NASB), he was describing this quantum leap from a self-controlled, enemy-dominated life into the very heart of our Father of Light.

When I was still in college, I wanted to fly to Philadelphia to visit my then-fiancée, Cathy. As a student, an airline was offering a cheap flight, so I decided to take advantage of the fares. But my parents were very traditional, Italian folks. They were great and loving parents but just old school. No son of theirs was going to go hurdling through the sky in a metal box way too heavy to fly. Though they were rife with fear, I made the flight. But I have to admit, they had given me a lot to pray about as I entered the plane. Something broke in me that day, however. Something far greater than just the experience of flying. I was determined to never allow someone's fear of anything to overtake me. There is a big difference between taking sound advice and falling under the influence of another's fear. A good sense of discernment always helps me to determine the difference between the two.

Make no mistake here. Israel's deliverance from Egypt to the Wilderness was a quantum leap for them. Everything was different. Everything changed. Their conversations in Egypt were all about brick making, the whip of the task master, the hope of deliverance one day, the struggle of simple survival. When they left Egypt, their conversations changed to songs of deliverance, views of pillars of smoke and fire, gathering manna, and, of course, whining and bickering about the wisdom of fleeing Egypt. Yes, a quantum leap is to the better. Nonetheless, these folks were too self-absorbed to perceive what their Father had actually done for them. They left slavery behind, but after the dust had cleared, all their human weaknesses were securely with them, blinding them from what had just happened and what was waiting for them.

Another Quantum Leap

When Israel crossed the River into the Promised Land, everything changed again. Another quantum leap once again changed their vision, their desires and perspectives. They now talked about having to plant fields, dig cisterns, plant vineyards, and conquer enemies. They no longer had manna falling from heaven; they now had to make their own bread. Their clothes began to wear out; they now had to make their own apparel. They no longer had pillars of smoke and fire to lead them. But at last, they would get to know their Father and learn His leading. Finally, they would begin to move forward and to understand their future. A change of this magnitude certainly was a quantum leap for them.

My Similar Journey

But the journey of Israel from Egypt to Canaan is far more than someone else's history. It is *our* journey. It is *my* personal journey. It is *your* personal journey. It is our personal journey from being a slave son to a maturing son, from a struggling son to an overcoming son, from a demanding prodigal son to a maturing and focused son.

I can relate to the Ancients. Like them, there was nothing I wanted more than to be free from the slavery to the things over which I had no control. I was every bit a slave to my sin as Israel was to the Egyptians. Back in those days, I had no choice. I simply was led like a dog on a leash to wherever my taskmasters (the fleshy side of me that wants only gratification and pleasure) wanted me to go. Sin and iniquity had complete control. It was an endless cycle of temptation, sin, and repeat. Failure mounted upon failure. My life was on an endless downward spiral. I had no idea where the bottom of that spiral would be, but I was definitely not looking forward to it!

Two Sacrifices

But then, the Lamb of God, Who was the Sacrifice and Deliverer, lead me from my Egypt as triumphantly, as completely, as finally as our Father had led Israel from Egypt. I experienced my own quantum leap. I was relocated, in a moment of time, from the domain, the control, the slavery of darkness and then miraculously placed on the road to my Promised Land. There, everything was new. My eyes saw things I had never seen. My ears heard things they had never heard. My heart leaped with a hope it had never even imagined was possible. My Father had sent me a Deliverer! Me! He sent His Son for me! It was a like a dream come true! "God is real!" I would shout to myself. "He is actually real!" Of course, I had no idea how to act, what to say, how to live, what to think. But like Miriam, all I could do was dance! I was free, indeed.

Soon after the initial euphoria passed, however, I discovered that not everything inside of me was happy with what had happened. Doubt, rebellion, and fear were there and became daily struggles. I didn't understand it. I was set free, but something was still very wrong. I was confused. I felt let down, like I had been just told a story. Sometimes I just wanted to go back—I missed the old way, the old thrills. I forgot that they were an endless cycle of pain and loneliness, that they were actually killing me. I forgot the heartache and only remembered what I thought were the "good times." Of course, the so-called good times always ended in disillusionment, sorrow, and pain. Nonetheless, I wanted it. I craved it. I would even say that I needed it. Needless to say, I wandered in my own Wilderness, making excuses for my feelings, creating doctrines to make it okay to feel the way I was feeling. The only problem—I was not growing. I was barely hanging on. All the study and prayer barely kept me alive. I begged for deliverance. I fasted for many, many days. I prayed. I claimed, demanded, and declared my freedom, my wholeness, only to have those words return to me empty and unfulfilled.

Some quantum leap! I left the place of bondage only to be trapped in a place of inner turmoil, confusion, uncertainty, and secret lusts. I left my Egypt to escape the sin I hated only to be trapped by the wanton sin I secretly craved. All the worship services and all-night prayer meetings did not have the power I needed. I could pray for the sick and they would be instantly healed. I could counsel the broken and see them made whole. I could prophesy, preach, and do all the awesome things that a good Pentecostal needed to do. But I was still a prisoner. I was tormented by the things within me that still demanded my attention.

There is little point to go on here about what my Wilderness was like. If you are honest, you can at least somewhat relate to this. Ultimately, I came to yet another place of decision—in spite of the forces working against me, the enemies that heckled me and kept me focused on them instead of my Father, I could not deny Him who lived inside of me and always urged me to go on.

The Quantum Leap into Death and Resurrection

So yes, here was another quantum leap. Here was another time when I would go from the reign of my fleshy fears and inner torments to the Kingdom that was ruled by my loving King. This leap would be as transformationally different as was leaving the slavery of sin. To leave Egypt meant to flee the bondage I hated. To leave the Wilderness, I would have to commit to leave the sin I wanted—a different sacrifice indeed. Like the sacrifice that freed me from Egypt, this sacrifice would also require a death, but this death would not be the Lamb of God. This death would be my own and I would have to commit to dying daily. For this death would be one in which I would once and for all defeat the torment of my sin and iniquity from my mind as Jesus had dismissed it from the control over my life. My death to these mind-numbing temptations and torments meant that I would no longer fear the doom of going back to the past. Rather, my life would be refocused to see that sin was preventing me from experiencing all that my Father has for me right now. That thought was more than I could bear, for I wanted Him in His fullness more than anything else.

Once I had made the determination to live in broken repentance, my life changed drastically. I had determined not to let sin rule my body, but I would have to live in brokenness to let that happen in my life. I now saw that the will of God was within my grasp if I was only willing to repent as many times as necessary. To hell with my pride; I would not allow my own false sense of superiority stop me anymore. His destiny became more important than my pride. Sin and iniquity were now the enemy of my future, not the magnet to go backward. In the Wilderness, my focus was on my needs, my wants, and my own desires. In Canaan, my focus is on Him no matter what the cost to my fleshy self. By focusing on heavenly things instead of earthy things, I discovered that temptation and iniquity were not able to have such a stranglehold in my life. Heaven was my destination, but it was my destiny right here and now that I became passionate about fulfilling.

It is still true today, make no mistake—when I allow my mind to wander into self-pity, selfish needs, and regrets, I open myself to the attacks of the enemy. When I choose to live where these thoughts and temptations live, I am now living in enemy-occupied territory. Surrendering that land to the King turns it back to the control of the King, expanding His Kingdom, His rule, and reign within my life.

But this is where it can get hard. It is not always easy to quickly, completely, and without excuse repent of the sin that sometimes so easily overpowers us. Many of us might be quicker to repent if we believed the sin was actually our own fault. But it is far easier to become a chronic accuser, willing to shift responsibility for our sin onto anyone or anything that might be involved in some way. Other times, if we are unable to find freedom for a particular sin, we might face the temptation to change our beliefs in order to accommodate our failures. This can lead to the creation of entire theologies that cover and allow for our weaknesses. In reality, it is always *me* who is first in need of prayer and repentance. It is *my* pride that must take the fall. If I have to repent a hundred times a day, so be it. I would rather see my pride broken than miss the opportunity of experiencing union with my Father.

Jesus famously dealt with our need to personally repent rather than accuse or blame others when He said:

> *And why do you look at the speck in your brother's eye, but do not consider the plank in your own eye? Or how can you say to your brother, "Let me remove the speck from your eye"; and look, a plank is in your own eye? Hypocrite! First remove the plank from your own eye* (Matthew 7:3-5).

I absolutely hate sin. The Christ in me absolutely hates sin. The best remedy to this dilemma is to go to Father with a sincere heart of repentance and a willingness to humble ourselves as often we need to. This is how we will never fall short of His glory: We simply recognize our sins quickly, thoroughly confess and repent of them—and move on. Honestly, if we were as determined to eradicate sin from our lives as we are determined to eradicate sickness and difficult circumstances, we would be far different people indeed.

Repentance, the Only Path into Victory

> *You have loved righteousness and hated lawlessness; therefore God, Your God, has anointed You with the oil of gladness more than Your companions* (Hebrews 1:9).

With this lifestyle of repentance, everything changed for me. I was no longer stuck in an endless circle of Wilderness drudgery. No longer would I come upon tracks in the sand that I had made myself when I passed on this same desert trail months and even years earlier. Now I was truly going somewhere. I was being made new. My mind was changing, resulting in changed words and desires, a changed outlook on life, and a new attitude toward others. The Son had set me free from my Egypt.

It is here, in my Promised Land, that I surrender and give myself to the Life of the King within. He is the one who scatters the enemy and silences the tormenting voices. He leads me in paths of righteousness through the heart of my Canaan where my daily obedience routs the giants and allows my King to reign in peace and joy. In that Land, He anoints me with the oil of gladness.

I AM a son. I know Him as my Father, and I am doing what I hear Him say to my heart. Sons inherit everything when they grow up. The prodigal received his money but missed the real inheritance—the image and likeness of his elder brother, Jesus Christ.

> *As for me, I will see Your face in righteousness; I shall be satisfied when I awake in Your likeness* (Psalm 17:15).

Questions for the Determined

1. How have you grown comfortable with life in the Wilderness? What sort of changes do you feel God is calling you to make so that you can inherit your Promised Land?

2. What are the "giants" that inhabit your land? How do they look in your eyes? How do you think God sees them?

3. How often have you gone through a death and resurrection process like the ones described in this chapter? What was the result? Is God calling you into another death and resurrection process?

Chapter 7

MATURING SONS

> My dear son,
> You are on a very private, very holy journey. It is true that most do not understand and most will try to resist what is happening within your heart. Nonetheless, the time has come for **some** to enter this most incredible experience of maturing sons as a way of life. Do not try to justify old doctrines or hold on to things that no longer fit your newly discovered way of living. This new life will continuously unfold. Just when you think you have come to the end of discovery, a brand-new beginning seems to come out of nowhere. The more you authentically surrender to what you discover, without holding anything back, the more He will show you. His eternal life is continuously rising in the hearts of the surrendered, the broken, the faithful, the quiet—you.

What is the picture of a maturing son? How will he be recognized in the earth? What will it be about him that will cause those around him to identify him as more than just another person, another preacher, another church member, another religious person? What, in fact, makes a son, a son?

To the Evangelical, a mature son is a faithful follower of the local church to which he belongs. He believes what he is told, works a full-time job, tithes as required, and gives offerings as asked. He is in the building almost every time the church is open and is a faithful servant to the house. He talks like everyone in the church, dresses like them, and votes like them. He relies heavily on the pastor and elders, calling on them to dedicate their children to the Lord, and at the right time baptizes them. The pastor will marry them, counsel them, and then bury them. This mature son of the house loves what the house loves and despises what they despise. He is a good witness to the community on behalf of the church and regularly serves where asked. These sons more or less evangelize, especially by inviting friends, neighbors, co-workers to services, especially revival week and family nights. A mature son in this house is truly a "good and faithful servant" to the local assembly, falling completely in line with the rules of church.

To a denominational believer, a mature son follows the rules, is not an embarrassment to the church, can be counted on to tithe and show up most Sundays. He is not evangelistic and does not openly express his faith. He is probably a generational member to at least a particular denomination if not a specific church in that denomination. He volunteers as he is asked and his lifestyle generally assures him of his personal salvation. He is seldom challenged from the pulpit. On the contrary, his presence is coveted by the leadership and little is said or done that could ruffle their peaceful co-existence. These sons are often pillars in the community and are respected by their peers.

To a Pentecostal or Charismatic, a mature son is filled with the Spirit, moves in the gifts of the Spirit, and believes in all the supernatural manifestations one can imagine. His church is relatively new on the scene, often meeting in a temporary setting. He is, most likely, a first- or second-generation believer and has a strong love for Jesus. To this person, the regular manifestation of miracles is a sure sign of walking in God's will. These sons dress very casually, carry their Bibles to service, and keep their judgment of others to a small circle of close "prayer warriors." They are ardent evangelists and work hard to show the love of God to those around them.

But What Does He Look Like?

But what does a maturing son of God really look like? If we are going to honestly study this question, we must honestly evaluate the life of Jesus without the added ideas of whatever contemporary Christian culture we belong to. We must be honest and not exclude some of things Jesus did because they are too radical. Shedding these outer religious adornments of man, denomination, and tradition is a task all by itself. Rooted deep in the heart of man is the need to control, build, maintain, and, of course, grow. The religious world has done its job in designing their various versions of Christianity in such a way as to maintain the "success" of their churches and denominations. Their goal, of course, is to continue the generational existence of their organizations. Nonetheless, an authentic son of God is most assuredly recognized by His uncanny inner resemblance to his Elder Brother, Jesus.

But what does Jesus look like in our day? What does it mean for a 21st-century son who wants nothing more than to have the Light of his Father shining through him? To find that answer, one must legitimately step away from the binding limitations of religion. For sons are as different from the world and from the religious system today as Jesus was from the world and the religious system when He walked the earth so long ago.

It is true that Jesus was offensive to the religious folks and was hated by those who saw His life as a real threat to the religious order of things. It is also true that He was considered a fool to the political class. He was ignored by the government as a lunatic and was considered absolutely no threat to the Roman Empire.

Among the religious, Jesus was not hated for arrogantly flaunting doctrine or carrying a holier-than-thou attitude, for He did neither. He did not come across like a multi-level marketing salesman just looking for someone new to hook and reel into the fold. He did not mislead, intimidate, or condemn. He was never condescendingly judgmental or exclusive. But He was offensive, nonetheless. His love made Him offensive. His love made Him stand out among men and their leaders. His love set a plumb line, a standard that separated Him from those whose words were eloquent but whose actions were less than stellar. He didn't try to be different. He just *was* different. His authentic compassion, compelling words of hope, and His unconditional love drew the masses. This was something that the religious elites of the day could never do for they did not have love as their controlling inner dynamic. He proved that love, in fact, that is not played out in the reality of daily life is not love at all. The religious enforced the strict rules of engagement set forth in their laws. But there was little room for anything else. The elite religious class watched with disdain as the masses suffered, starved, and strove to obey what their leaders themselves could never do and then, after a lifetime of struggle, finally died.

But love broke the walls of division and class, as it always does. Love puts everything on a level plain. Love does not judge first but gives first, as Jesus did, giving His life for a fallen race before a single person repented. Love responds first, gathers first, hopes first, forgives first. Love does not react. Love initiates. Love assumes the best and offers the most. It opens its heart and refuses to condemn. It sees the deepest part of the heart and does not respond to outward appearances, attitudes, or opinions. Love breaks through the hardness of hate, the pain of separation, and the finality of death. Love, the most powerful force in the universe, was contained in a single person, the Son of God. The Son showed us how Life would be for anyone who yields to love's overwhelming reality of ultimate joy. The Son, this Christ of God, willingly shares this love with anyone who will surrender to its mystical but tangible reality.

Authentic sons are the foundational stability for any society that wants to endure. Sons are spiritual statesmen whose lives encourage those who are pure in heart, those with no need to control. Their righteous standard, their love-initiated, love-guided, love-taught and love-fulfilled lifestyle is the standard and portal through which the world can clearly see the unfettered, unencumbered Christ of God. When the world sees our Elder Brother through us, it sees tangible compassion and love that causes them to dare hope again. Sons just love, gather, bless, and encourage. Any miracle that flows from sons flows from a heart that is driven, motivated, and surrendered to the King who indwells them.

Jesus, our Elder Brother, is called the "anchor for the soul." This Anchor makes Him the Anchor within those who surrender to Him, and they in turn become the anchors in the earth through whom His Kingdom is established. They are the beachheads of love and moral standards on the planet. This sense, this "knowing" is not a matter of correct doctrine, correct theology, or the correct denomination. It is the result of an inner assurance that is born out of an interactive friendship with God.

Without a building, without the approval of the leaders, without the trappings of tradition, Jesus loved, gathered, fed, taught, healed, and loved some more. He ate with sinners and sat with drunks and prostitutes. His love broke down walls of fear and condemnation erected by religious gatekeepers. No wonder they hated Him. His Life spelled hope for the faithful who simply wanted to know they were loved, that they could find God and walk with Him, that He would forgive and transform them. But this same Life spelled doom for those who hearts were hard, whose opinions were narrow, and whose piety was rigid. Everything that genuine love proves, indeed, is offensive to those who have no plumb line, no destiny, and no standard of living other than their own meandering attitudes and uncertain morality. The stable and secure ones who are driven by Divine love will always be hated by those who will not allow the King to influence their lives.

The picture of Jesus as painted for us in the gospels is our best written example of how Jesus lived, loved, and encouraged the people around Him—and He has not changed since He walked the earth 2,000 years ago.

Jesus Christ is the same yesterday, today, and forever (Hebrews 13:8).

As we learn to yield to our Elder Brother within our hearts, we also become a hands-on demonstration of His love and reality in the world. His gathering heart is still building the individual and drawing him to the wide-open arms of our loving Father. And our Father is still building His Kingdom in the hearts and lives of individuals who yield to Him. He does these things not by virtue of control and intimidation, but by His love. This is the way His Kingdom has always worked and will continue to work.

When I Stood, I Fell

Some have become frustrated with the lack of transformation, authentic change, and measurable progress in their lives. Their exasperation leads them to believe that the fault must be God's because they have done everything they could and followed everything they have been taught and still came up short. I understand that. I have been there too.

I remember times when I did all to stand and yet still fell—it was awful. Where was the promise of God? When I did all to stand, I still failed my God, myself, and those I love. Why?

It is amazing that men will point their finger at God before examining themselves and those who have led them thus far. Have we considered that we might be on the wrong path, that we might be following those who are leading us on a journey that just continuously loops around the Wilderness? Many of us are too willing to "hear" anything that absolves us of responsibility. There is always someone willing to offer destructive advice to us. I've learned that the most difficult issue I have to deal with is *myself*. I am ultimately responsible for who I choose to follow, whether it be a preacher, denomination, a movement, my own way of thinking, or the enemy.

Maybe we are doing all we have been told to do but things are not going like we were told they would. In this case, we need to remember that God is for us, not against us. No matter what we are going through, blame, anger, and offense against Him is fruitless for us. We must repent of our anger toward Him and find Him for ourselves. As we do, we will awaken again to the truth that He is always set on helping us. There is destiny in His heart for us. He has only good in store for us. There is unshakable resolve in His heart to bring us into the dream He has for us.

I am convinced that God gives us roadblocks to get us to the point of exasperation so we question what we were told and then finally find the courage to venture out into the things God has specifically spoken to us—even if they are not readily acceptable to others. For me, as I began to break free from bad advice and grow in confidence in my relationship with Him, I finally discovered that God had a path for me that did not fit the plans of the "collective." His path seldom does.

Experience Is the Missing Element

Our personal experience adds credibility to our lives, as it should. So many students graduate from Bible school and are ready to set the world on fire for God only to discover that a leader is not made in a classroom and success in life is not gauged by test scores. It is in the crucible of life that ordinary folks become extraordinary. It is through enduring the extremes of emotion that are born of failure and the rejection of those we trusted the most that the "average" believer is elevated to "excellent." It is here that the arrogant is reduced to brokenness and the self-assured reduced into a dependency that God can use.

In the Outer Court and Holy Place, God breaks Himself down into components we can understand. In the Most Holy Place, man is broken down into components God can use. In the Outer Court and Holy Place, the unbroken man sees God in His personal attributes. In the Most Holy Place, the broken man sees God in all His fullness of glory. We would do well not to be so quick to rebuke, discard, or dismiss the very trials that God sends to us for our perfection. Rather than our first inclination to run from difficulties, we should take the time to hear what it is we may learn from such times. Indeed, it is a shame to waste our sorrows. In fact, Peter tells us to rejoice in them, for they are proving the genuineness of our faith!

> *In this you greatly rejoice, though now for a little while, if need be, you have been grieved by various trials, that the genuineness of your faith, being much more precious than gold that perishes, though it is tested by fire, may be found to praise, honor, and glory at the revelation of Jesus Christ* (1 Peter 1:6-7).

Maturing Sons

Some of you remember the original ROTC military enlistment program. It was an accelerated course in officer training and combat-readiness. The course was exhaustive in all points of study except actual combat experience. The young men were educated and thrown into leadership roles on the battlefield even though they were just out of training. Of course, the results were a disaster. No one would follow someone who did not have the experience of actual warfare. No one would risk their lives under the command of someone who had never known the fear of battle, the pressure of being under fire, or the trust required to obey an officer without second-guessing him.

Our secular educational system also knows that graduation does not, in itself, qualify someone for anything more than an entry position in a company. We are only prepared for greater responsibility as our experience increases.

Many years ago, I attended a motivational seminar. My desire was to review the program and possibly use it for those who worked at my company. The motivational founder was not going to attend, so the cost was much less as his surrogate did not have the experience of the founder. When we arrived, we heard that the surrogate had taken ill and would not be there. The start of the seminar was delayed for over an hour as we all wondered if the event would be cancelled or another person would teach the classes. We were pleasantly surprised to hear the name of the founder announced as the replacement.

The conference was amazing. We were elated to be taught by the originator, the one with the vision, the one who developed the material, the one who had tested it in his own life. It was an awesome lesson! Who do you want to teach you? Someone who has studied the material or the one who developed it? The one who studied a person's life or the person himself? No wonder the scripture says:

> *When Jesus had finished these words, the crowds were amazed at His teaching; for He was teaching them as one having authority, and not as their scribes* (Matthew 7:28-29 NASB).

What gives a person authority? Is it a university degree or a Bible school certificate? Is it physical appearance, presentation, or personality? These may all play a part to dazzle those who have no discernment, but they certainly do not impress the authentically hungry.

> *Now as they* [Jewish elders] *observed the confidence of Peter and John and understood that they were uneducated and untrained men, they were amazed, and began to recognize them as having been with Jesus* (Acts 4:13 NASB).

It is amazing to me how simple this is. The learned scribes, Pharisees, and Sadducees with all their titles, adornments, and ceremonies did not have the authority Jesus carried, the Son of a carpenter dressed in a peasant's robe and followed by sinners. Ironically, the common folks could see right through those leaders. The folks saw the shallowness of their religious rulers and easily turned to follow the One whose authority was delivered through Divine experience.

The difference between the "religious" and the "real" is simple and obvious to those who are hungry for God. Those who have been with Jesus, who are with Him, who yield to Him have an unmistakable humility and authority that cannot be duplicated. Their love and compassion is unmistakable.

What Is a Son Apart from His Father?

> *What is man that You are mindful of him, and the son of man that You visit him? For You have made him a little*

lower than the angels, and You have crowned him with glory and honor (Psalm 8:4-5).

Most of us do not get it. God sees us as far more than we see ourselves. After all, He sees us as we are and what He has destined us to be. Most of us see ourselves through the limitations of human understanding and the dismal picture painted of us by those who have never seen Him and have no idea what it means to be a maturing son. It is quite a shame. We have listened to so many for so long telling us why we cannot be who we feel we are and why we will never become anything more than we are now. By now, most of us have been sufficiently indoctrinated to believe what we were told to believe. It's such a pity. The fate of the planet is literally in the hands of those "made lower than the angels" and yet we live so small, expect so little, and sacrifice nothing. Have we lost the vision of our calling to grow up into Christ? Don't we know that we are meant to be the "hands and feet" of the Lord on the earth? Did we forget that we will judge angels?

Meanwhile, "shortcut Christianity" continues to experiment with religious formulas and dabble in Divine deal-making as though our destiny is a bargaining chip that can be negotiated to get what we want from God. I will say it again—those who live this way are in a typical Wilderness existence. This kind of living can never be anything but confusing, directionless, hopeless, and eventually unbearably uncomfortable. It leaves us paupers spiritually, emotionally, and financially.

Even the best that the Wilderness had to offer kept the Ancients wandering on the wrong side of their Father's ultimate intention for them. They knew how to gather manna, carry water, break down camp, and set it up again. They knew how to set fires, gather by tribes, and bury their dead. They knew everything they needed to know to survive. They even saw amazing miracles. But none of it brought them to the destiny they wanted. None of it helped them to build a Kingdom.

None of it helped them accumulate the wealth that they would need to become a nation. Spiritual, emotional, and financial growth would not be possible on the wrong side of the River.

Kingdoms are not grown through block grants. Nations do not become great unless the citizens of that nation put their hand to the plow to make a kingdom strong. Crossing the Jordan would mean that there would be no more manna, no endless water supply, and no meat. There would be no canopy to cool them by day or pillar of fire to warm them by night. They would have to be responsible. They would have to work. Their self-centered, personal protectionism would have to give way to the greater good. They would have to relinquish the seductive, false safety of Wilderness life in order to experience the fullness of life that awaited them just on the other side of their obedience.

Yes, for this motley crew to ever become more than just a wandering mass of people in a Wilderness that they never conquered, they would have to change. They would have to *want* what their Father was offering them. Simply put, they would have to grow up.

It is here, between the Wilderness and the Promised Land, that the division between the prodigals and the maturing sons becomes evident. As the Ancients demonstrated to us, it is the maturing sons who will inherit everything while the demanding and complaining rebellious will end up losing everything.

> *Moreover, brethren, I do not want you to be unaware that all our fathers were under the cloud, all passed through the sea, all were baptized into Moses in the cloud and in the sea, all ate the same spiritual food, and all drank the same spiritual drink. For they drank of that spiritual Rock that followed them, and that Rock was Christ. But with most of them God was not well pleased, for their bodies were scattered in the wilderness.*

> *Now these things became our examples, to the intent that we should not lust after evil things as they also lusted. And do not become idolaters as were some of them. As it is written, "The people sat down to eat and drink, and rose up to play." Nor let us commit sexual immorality, as some of them did, and in one day twenty-three thousand fell; nor let us tempt Christ, as some of them also tempted, and were destroyed by serpents; nor complain, as some of them also complained, and were destroyed by the destroyer. Now all these things happened to them as examples, and they were written for our admonition, upon whom the ends of the ages have come* (1 Corinthians 10:1-11).

Though every believer is a son, few choose to go on to experience the full extent of Kingdom citizenry. Maturing sonship is afforded to the sober-minded son who is not building for himself but for the generations to follow him. We already have had enough ROTC-trained spiritual leaders. God is looking for those who know that they cannot carry His mantle of authority until they have cut covenant with God by sacrifice.

Circumcised Hearts

Coming out of Egypt, the Lamb cut covenant with us by His own sacrifice. Now we cut covenant with Him as we offer ourselves in daily surrender to Him in the deepest, most protected places in our hearts where no one sees but us.

This not a new thing God is doing. This experience is not locked in time as though prepared for only now. He has been showing Himself to His own for centuries, waiting for those who would hear Him in the deepest part of their heart. God help us to hear what He is saying to His sons.

Therefore circumcise the foreskin of your heart, and be stiff-necked no longer (Deuteronomy 10:16).

So, what does a maturing son look like and how recognizable is he within your own heart? You are the only one who can honestly answer that question. But one thing is for certain, He who began this great, supernatural work in you is determined to bring it to its logical conclusion—you, expressing His fullness in your everyday life.

Sanctify yourselves, for tomorrow the Lord will do wonders among you (Joshua 3:5).

Questions for the Courageous

1. Have you made a "covenant with the Lord by sacrifice"? What does *your* heart look like when it is circumcised to the Lord?

2. Have you ever had to step out from under leadership that was taking you in the wrong direction to honestly follow the direction the Lord was leading you in? What was the result?

3. Where are you right now in your life—Wilderness wandering or entering the Promised Land?

Chapter 8

Everything Else Is Less

My dear son,

   Honesty with yourself and with God, in the deepest part of your heart, is the way to true and authentic freedom. The deceiver can only accuse if he sees something hidden from God. If there is nothing there, the vanquished foe has nothing to whine about. No wonder Jesus said, "The prince of this world is coming and he has no hold over me." Want to shut his worthless mouth? Stay honest before God! Now you are truly free. With this kind of heart purity, there is no end to what God can and will do to you, in you, and through you. Once again, you win.

> *Beware lest anyone cheat you through philosophy and empty deceit, according to the tradition of men, according to the basic principles of the world, and not according to Christ.*
> —Colossians 2:8

The foundations of humanity's man-made attempts to reach God are shaken when simple folks like you and I begin to understand not just who we are, but *why* we are. Once we begin to make this momentous discovery, everything changes. Self-discovery is most essential to a maturing people, for no one else can really tell us who we are. They can only confirm it. We must find it first within. For the freedom to explore the boundless possibilities that God has placed within the human soul is the greatest threat that controlling powers face. When man begins to respond as a son to his Father, the control, intimidation and power once levied against the masses begins to erode and is ultimately replaced by a Father-son relationship that cannot be usurped by title, promotion, bribe, or even brute force.

The very foundations of any society are built on the notion that man is essentially a follower of the stronger man, that he basically does not have the wherewithal to function apart from the close supervision of a superior class, an educated, anointed, predetermined elite few who will call the shots for the rest of us who do not know any better. Unfortunately, the past millennia have all but proven this to be true—and it will continue to be true until the sons of God arise, until the redeemed of the Lord hear the sound of their Father's Voice and believe, accept, and act upon who He says they really are. For there is no one more dangerous to the established system of government, science, media, or religion than the person who knows who he is and what he can accomplish with a soft, attentive heart; hard work; and focused attention. The future is written by those who get there first, understand it first, and are willing to risk everything for the vision they hold in their heart.

Tomorrow is not beholden to anyone in particular. It simply yields to the ones who are willing to make the sacrifices necessary to see the world changed—and it will change into the image of those who carry the authority to change it. The little worlds we make will inevitably reflect the image of those who create them. Across the spectrum of human thought and philosophy, many so-called leaders are merely egotists driven to impose their image on others. But whether their "authority to lead" was stolen, earned, bestowed, or bought, such forces can powerfully influence and even control the lives of others.

The entrenched rulers of religion and society who seek to control the masses to their own particular view of a world order are not necessarily entitled by any universal decree, Divine will, or governmental guarantee. Their assumptions of superiority over others give them a sense of entitlement to maintain their positions of unquestioned and unchallenged power. As long as the masses are willing to be the vessels of oligarchic control, whether that control is religious or secular, little will actually change on this earth. Most people are the willing and obedient subjects of those to whom they have submitted.

Please make no mistake, these ruthless leaders control political parties, organized religion, and certainly much of the media and entertainment industry. Subjugation to their whims is the downfall of any society. Maturing sons must arise with courage and commitment.

"Need" Focused

We know that...the whole world lies under the sway of the wicked one (1 John 5:19).

The ruling class floods the minds and hearts of the folks with frivolous issues, distracting them from the thing that would release them into the very plan that has been destined for them since before the earth was born. The average person allows himself to be so inundated with the worthless and mundane that he has no time to actually think for himself or to develop his own sense of identity, purpose, or destiny. Maturing sons will silence their world that they might hear the words of the King from within.

To varying degrees, all earthly governments inevitably end up with a system that enslaves the masses in one way or another. Often, these political leaders do this by making the people think they need a "big brother" to watch over them, to make life-altering decisions for them, to spend their money, to care for them from birth to death.

Religious oligarchs preach freedom from sin and freedom to "become"—as long the masses don't become greater than those in charge. These leaders contend that they must maintain their positional authority or chaos will ensue. Therefore, keeping the masses in the confines of a system that ensures control from one generation to the next is essential. But a quick look over the landscape of life will prove that chaos has always been rampant among religions as well as secular governments. Their humanist efforts are simply leading us in a downward spiral of destruction. So while demanding obedience for the sake of societal order is exactly what is missing, the free will of the people to determine their own destiny is sacrificed to the controlling powers over them.

Interpreting Scripture to their own advantage, religious shepherds of the flock convince believers of their anointed position over the more simple folks. But whether they are sincere, weak-minded, unlearned, or too busy to hear their King for themselves, the average believer is duped into a subservient position in relation to leaders who keep them in check, under control, and serving the needs of those who rule them.

The religious ruling class is often so concerned for their own political and financial security that the destiny of the believer takes second place. These leaders have created a religious social welfare class for themselves where they are the ones who are pampered, served, and almost worshiped. But the authentic five-fold minister remembers the last lesson of their Elder Brother when He took a bowl of water and a towel, got down on His knees, and washed the feet of those He had taught for three years. The demonstration was much more than a metaphorical teaching. Christ-yielded leaders are meant to be servants in deeds, not only in words. If the Christ of God could serve the least, the last, and the lost, how much more should we?

> *But Jesus called them to Himself and said, "You know that the rulers of the Gentiles lord it over them, and their great men exercise authority over them. It is not this way among you, but whoever wishes to become great among you shall be your servant, and whoever wishes to be first among you shall be your slave; just as the Son of Man did not come to be served, but to serve, and to give His life a ransom for many"* (Matthew 20:25-28 NASB).

The Church that Jesus is building is being built by Jesus. This is not very deep. Christ-yielded leaders work under the command of Him who releases destiny as He sees fit and according the dream that the King has in His heart for the individual.

It is not usually the weakness of the believer but rather the control of those over them that prevents God's will from being accomplished through the believer. Hence, the religious system fumbles and falters through time, generationally becoming less effective, resorting to secular political power to get their way because the real power within them is lost. Our growth "from glory to glory" is never experienced by most. It is a sorry state of affairs, to be sure. All hope would be lost if it were not for the unshakable purpose of our Father, continuously rising from those who can hear beyond the prattle of religious and secular humanism. These folks will prophesy what few will venture to declare. The King is most certainly coming through His sons. Therefore, maturing sons proclaim another allegiance. They follow a different Captain. The Kingdom to which they submit the affairs of life is the one from within. The King they worship is already enthroned on the only Throne that counts—the one in their heart.

Sons First

In light of the systems that would seek to hold Him down, it is important to affirm who we really are:

I AM a son first—a maturing son. Everything else about me is less important than this supreme fact. Any title, position, or power given by man is worth far less. I am in process. That is, I recognize my propensity to do my own will, fulfill my own secret needs and desires. Therefore, I recognize that I have not arrived to the place of the maturity I want or God wants.

I AM a maturing son. I am living a lifestyle of "broken repentance." To the best of my ability, I am allowing my King to bring conviction to my heart along with the grace to quickly and without excuse, repent.

I AM a maturing son. I am walking with those I know have my best interests at heart. I can trust them because we have walked difficult miles together. Our love has been proven in the fires of testing and struggle. We walk as peers but submit to one another in love and in the fear of the Lord, allowing turmoil and suffering to meld our hearts together as one. We are family, having made a sacrificial covenant when all others accused and deserted. These are the only ones who have access to my heart, my life, my destiny. This is not a talking point. It is life and death.

I AM a maturing son. I diligently embrace a lifestyle that maintains humility, compassion, patience, and love. I want to experience broken repentance as a lifestyle. And when I see the things within me that must change, I run to my King for mercy, knowing that He will forgive and continuously empower me to go on.

I AM a maturing son. I have no delusions of grandeur, no inflated sense of who I AM apart from Him. For if the circumstances of everyday life taught me anything, it is that I am what I am only because God has allowed it. I have nothing that belongs to another, nothing to inflate my ego, and absolutely nothing worth living for or dying for apart from the reality of who I AM before God. I AM His son.

Which Son Are You?

As mentioned earlier, we are born as sons. We do not become a son. But we only become a *maturing* son, one who is able to soberly administrate the inheritance entrusted to us as we grow in surrendered obedience to our Father. Whether that inheritance is money, position, talent, or any number of things, it has its greatest effect when it is handled by a maturing son. This is what the world is desperate for. It awaits sons of integrity, trustworthiness, and faithfulness. The world awaits statesmen.

Those who carry the mantle of "authority" without the lifestyle of a maturing son do more harm to our King than good. Although the "Seven Mountain Mandate" is popular, there is something far more basic, far more essential than taking these places of authority on the earth. My own heart must be conquered. My own heart must be surrendered to the King. Any authority granted apart from an authentically surrendered life is a heretical representation of the King's life in the earth. If I am not a maturing son, I have no right, authority, or place to oversee things that I know nothing about, let alone have experienced.

Seven Mountains or not, my heart is the principle mountain of authority that must be surrendered to the King. All our hearts must be soft, teachable, changeable, reflective as the King transforms our secret places of uncertainty and sin into the mountain of the Lord that the nations will run to. It is a lifelong endeavor, for sure. I am always most effective when I am most yielded and attentive to the King. It is He who is always at work transforming me into a more accurate representation of the Son. I want to be a visible and accurate picture of the love and compassion of my Lord the Light that shines with purity and hope, warmth and Life. A lamp is only as useful as it is clean. A dirty lampshade inhibits the light. The brightness of my Light to reach the masses around me is directly related to the cleanliness of my lampshade. Until my "mountain" is fully conquered by Him, any other mountain I conquer will be short-lived. Until then, I expect correction, instruction, and transformation from Him. This lifestyle will continue until I breathe my last breath. I am no longer content with "doing" the will of God anymore. I want to *be* the will of God.

False Shepherds

I've been around the block. I have seen more than my share of Charismatic leaders who are nothing more than prodigal sons and false shepherds. They may say they represent their Father, yet they forcefully declare the scriptures that demand submission to them and require obedience, honor, and financial support. In so doing, they actually discredit, destroy, and derail the purposes of God for individuals and ultimately those under their sphere of influence. This kind of immature ranting is in itself the primary indicator that they are occupying a position for which they are unqualified. Simply put, this is not how Jesus led. In fact, he warned against such leadership:

> *Then Jesus said to them, "Take heed and beware of the leaven of the Pharisees and the Sadducees"* (Matthew 16:6).
>
> *Then Jesus spoke to the multitudes and to His disciples, saying: "The scribes and the Pharisees sit in Moses' seat. Therefore whatever they tell you to observe, that observe*

and do, but do not do according to their works; for they say, and do not do. For they bind heavy burdens, hard to bear, and lay them on men's shoulders; but they themselves will not move them with one of their fingers. But all their works they do to be seen by men. They make their phylacteries broad and enlarge the borders of their garments. They love the best places at feasts, the best seats in the synagogues, greetings in the marketplaces, and to be called by men, 'Rabbi, Rabbi.' But you, do not be called 'Rabbi'; for One is your Teacher, the Christ, and you are all brethren. Do not call anyone on earth your father; for One is your Father, He who is in heaven. And do not be called teachers; for One is your Teacher, the Christ. But he who is greatest among you shall be your servant. And whoever exalts himself will be humbled, and he who humbles himself will be exalted" (Matthew 23:1-12).

Authentic Spiritual Maturity

Authentic spiritual maturity is not the product of years. It is not the kind of maturity taught by this world or sanctioned by its governments. It is taught by example and infused into the heart of every man through love. It is lived out by those who, themselves, have become mature sons of God as they walk out their own journey through life. It is how they live and it is why they are who they are. They have seen their existence apart from God and did not like it one bit. But rather than crumbling at this vision of their fallen nature, they run to Him for transformation, for healing, and for personal recovery. They surrender to Him every moment of every day. They begin to see themselves as truly Blood bought and eternally grateful for the Cross in all its ugliness and pain. Their difficult times and failures have proven to them that they can never save themselves or live the life that would qualify them for God's love. Theirs is a maturity learned in the turbulence of daily life as the difficult times are sorted out in the secrecy of the prayer closet and lived out in the crucible of human experience.

In "broken repentance," a truly transformational miracle begins to occur. In this place, pride begins to crumble, hate melts, and arrogance is shunned. In Him, stubbornness finds its end, the tongue of the slanderer is silenced, lusts no longer rule the day, and the distractions of this mortal realm are fervently resisted.

This process causes us to see others as we see ourselves and it becomes very apparent to us just where we would be without His grace. Our deepest heart's desire changes from one of self-promotion to a pattern of hiding in Christ, from controlling others to releasing them to their own destiny, from wanting their money to wanting their success, from desperately trying to be the center of attention to being content in the place God has put us.

We are sons by our spiritual DNA, but we are only made into mature sons through our obedience to Him in the deepest part of our hearts where no one sees the real battle that rages within us. Yes, authentic maturity is the Divine plan that turns us from immature sons into those who can rule with meekness, love, and compassion. These sons are a unique breed of human. But then, so was our King as He walked the earth. He is the same as He has always been as He lives His life through maturing sons.

Kingdom Leadership

The Scriptures carefully lay out the characteristics of true leaders—those who love, serve, sacrifice, and risk everything for the sake of the Church that Jesus is building. To all believers, whether leaders or beginners, His direction to us is the same:

Do nothing from selfish ambition or conceit, but in humility count others more significant than yourselves. Let each of you look not only to his own interests, but also to the interests of others. Have this mind among yourselves, which is yours in Christ Jesus, who, though he was in the form of God, did not count equality with God a thing to be grasped, but emptied himself, by taking the form of a servant, being born in the likeness of men (Philippians 2:3-7 ESV).

I AM a son. Everything else certainly pales in comparison to what it truly means to have God as my Father. My assurance, my confidence, and my place in the universe is complete because of who I AM. Any other title, position, function, or award can now come or go. It is of no consequence. I know who I AM. I know who my Father is, and I know His hand is always upon me for good. I will say it again—I AM a son.

Questions for the Courageous

1. Who is it that fits the description of this chapter as one you would follow? Who is it that you really want to follow?

2. Have you ever exhibited the kind of leadership and attitude that does not reflect the nature of your King? How did you see it and repent of it?

3. Do you recognize the work of the King in your life in a very personal, private way? Can you see that He wants you to be a reflection of His nature, His character? What opportunities are before you in which you can serve as a true son?

Chapter 9

SONS DRINK THE CUP

My dear son,

It is way too easy to see the apparent progress of another while you seem to be wallowing in the mire of human struggle and frustration. But you are not on their journey and they are not on yours. The road map with your name on it is uniquely yours. I am taking you somewhere that is as unique as you are. Don't second-guess the journey and do not judge yourself unworthy. That would be a terrible disservice and a bitter end to the powerfully beautiful work I am doing for you, in you, and through you. Stay the course, My beloved son. I can't wait for you to see what is just down the road, if you persevere.

Then the mother of the sons of Zebedee came to Jesus with her sons, bowing down and making a request of Him. And He said to her, "What do you wish?" She said to Him, "Command that in Your kingdom these two sons of mine may sit one on Your right and one on Your left." But Jesus answered, "You do not know what you are asking. Are you able to drink the cup that I am about to drink?" They said to Him, "We are

able." *He said to them, "My cup you shall drink; but to sit on My right and on My left, this is not Mine to give, but it is for those for whom it has been prepared by My Father." And hearing this, the ten became indignant with the two brothers. But Jesus called them to Himself and said, "You know that the rulers of the Gentiles lord it over them, and their great men exercise authority over them. It is not this way among you, but whoever wishes to become great among you shall be your servant, and whoever wishes to be first among you shall be your slave; just as the Son of Man did not come to be served, but to serve, and to give His life a ransom for many."*
—Matthew 20:20-28 NASB

There is no better way to say it. Sons drink the cup. They do not pass it along to someone else. They do not ask another to do for them what they are responsible to do for themselves. Sons pay their own way. They do not expect something for nothing. David would not make a sacrifice on land given to him. David was a son. Jacob took only spotted lambs from his father-in-law lest someone would say Laban made him great. Jacob was a son. Abraham paid for ground where Sarah was buried. Abraham was a son. Paul worked with his own hands so as to not burden the Church. Paul was a son. Sons do not expect to receive anything they did not earn or wield any authority for which they did not pay a comparable price.

Sons carry the weight and responsibility of their own "becoming." They embrace their Father within and confront the resistance of the carnal man without. They do not run from hardship; they eat it for lunch. They do not resist the King's insistence that they must change.

Rather, they surrender to change even when they do not understand. They surrender even when it hurts and, yes, even when they hate it. Like an athlete preparing for an Olympic game, sons are focused, committed, and attentive. Their satisfaction is in their obedience. Their hope is in the power of their Father, and their triumph is in their union with Him as He lives His life freely through them.

Maturing sons have no time for games, religious antics, or Pentecostal parlor tricks. They have no time and no interest in being a groupie for the latest revivalist. Sons are "becoming" manifest in the earth and have no need or interest in being on someone else's cutting edge. They understand that God's own work within them is the cutting edge to which they must be attentive.

Getting Our Attention

The power of transformation cannot be underestimated. Only a fool would think that he has figured God out. Only a fool would think that there is nothing within him that needs to change. However, there is often a vast difference between what we know in our head and how we actually live! A small and self-satisfied view of both God and ourselves will keep us from authentic relationship, authentic transformation, and real union with our King. We will end up living with caricatures of God and ourselves rather than the real deal. In turn, this will make us more susceptible to being duped by an American 21st-century version of Christianity that confuses the work of Jesus on the Cross with a "get out of jail free card" that negates the need for our own self-denial and resolve to take the personal responsibility for our actions and attitudes. But maturing sons have a different attitude.

Far from looking for ways to avoid conflict, these folks see difficulties as messengers from their King. They understand that He is merely using difficulties to get their attention. They know that when we cannot hear Him in our hearts, He will get our attention any way He can. He strives with us on many levels in hopes that we will eventually respond to Him so that He might lead us in the Way more accurately.

Of course, the more we are convinced that we are already on the most accurate way, the harder it is for Him to get through to us. Jesus spoke of this principle to the religious leaders of His day:

> *And Jesus said, "For judgment I have come into this world, that those who do not see may see, and that those who see may be made blind." Then some of the Pharisees who were with Him heard these words, and said to Him, "Are we blind also?" Jesus said to them, "If you were blind, you would have no sin; but now you say, 'We see.' Therefore your sin remains"* (John 9:39-41).

Is My Quiet Time with My King Really Quiet?

I hope you do not find my questions offensive. I have found (many times painfully) that the only way to satisfy the longing of my soul for my King is to be brutally honest with myself, knowing that He is the forgiving, loving, compassionate Person I have come to know. These are not merely His attributes "on paper" or merely doctrine I am asked to believe. Rather, I *know* these are His attributes because He has proven His character to me time and time again in the harsh realities of everyday life. Knowing His trustworthiness, I want to be in constant communion with Him, even when it means I may hear some things about myself that are not very pleasant.

For me, our Elder Brother always seems to get my attention in the quietness of my prayer closet. When I do not take the prayer time needed, He does not have that avenue to get my attention. Reading a daily devotional, while serving to bring the Scriptures before us every day, is not the same as waiting attentively in an attitude of quiet expectation. I have often found that taking away the daily devotional, turning off the worship music, putting down the latest book on prayer, and simply waiting on Him in silence offers me the best opportunity to hear from Him. But it seems humanity does not want to be alone with their thoughts. Silence intimidates us. Or is it that humanity does not want to be alone with Divine thoughts? It is amazing how many ways we have found to keep the noise level high enough to drown out any sounds we don't want to hear. With all the portable technology available to humanity, we don't ever have to really be alone or wrestle with waiting in silence.

Most want to hear His promises, get His prophetic words to us, and listen to messages about how we should be encouraged about everything. But I've discovered that spiritual growth requires more than that. It takes a serious-minded commitment to want to hear Him when He is speaking things that are not as easy to hear.

One Set of Ears

Several years ago, automobile companies developed a new sound buffering technology that made the inside of a car extremely quiet. The sound buffers took out 99 percent of the outside noise. The concept became an instant success. Who, after all, wanted a noisy car? Who doesn't want the random ruckus of the world blocked from their ears? But the problem was only realized later. The buffering technology that kept out what we didn't want to hear also kept out what we needed to hear in order to drive safely. Driving down a busy highway while oblivious to the sounds and activity around you may sound good, but it is most dangerous and for obvious reason. When this was discovered, the struggle between the comfort developers, the marketing departments, and car safety requirements was real indeed. How do you keep out one sound but not another? How do you block what you don't want to hear while not blocking the very things you need to hear that can keep you alive? The conclusion was that the sound buffers needed to be modified so that the driver could be aware of the possible trouble around him.

The truth is, we are a lot like that new sound buffering technology. We only have one set of ears. We cannot selectively turn off our spiritual listening. That is, we cannot have it both ways. If we drown out the convicting Voice of the King, we also drown out His comforting Voice as well. If we don't want to hear what needs to be changed, we will also be unable to hear when He wants to bless, encourage, and guide us. It is a relationship that He wants, after all. He is not our servant, our butler, or an online delivery service. He is our Father and we are sons. Like our Elder Brother, Jesus, we should only be seeking to do the things we see our Father doing.

And yes, that is a frightening proposition. It is true that unless we have been listening attentively to everything He wants to say, hearing Him again for the first time after however-many years will be unnerving. But He is gracious, compassionate, kind in His dealings with us. When we finally allow Him to drop the plumb line of Jesus next to us, He gives us grace, mercy, and the power to begin the inner changes that will allow His Light to shine through us like the first rays of dawn streak across the morning sky.

> *And so we have the prophetic word confirmed, which you do well to heed as a light that shines in a dark place, until the day dawns and the morning star rises in your hearts* (2 Peter 1:19).

The "fire of God" that warms the heart is the same fire that burns away the "wood, hay, and stubble" of the fleshy heart of man. Our lifestyle of broken repentance provides the fuel that the fire burns. This, likewise, is not very deep, folks. We cannot have light and warmth without fire. We cannot have a consistent fire without tossing fuel into it. The burnable kindling of our waywardness is the moment-by-moment source of the stuff that keeps the Fire of God burning within. This fire cannot be kept burning by worship, fasting, prayer, giving, or serving. It is maintained by humble, surrendered transformation within our hearts.

Of course, this is not to say that fasting and prayer have no place. But fasting or prayer in lieu of repentance does not change the inner man. It is just too easy to substitute a method or a process for the real need to respond to our Father directly and personally. The difference is subtle, yet profound—and the motivation of the heart is always the primary issue. If I fast and pray in place of simply doing what I need to do, or to manipulate God, I am wasting my time. But if my fasting and prayer is to create a quiet atmosphere of listening to Him, it will undoubtedly succeed.

Those who understand the need for personal, daily interaction and union with their Father will find little to argue to about in these words. Repetitive ritual too easily usurps the sacred place of genuine union with God. Prayer vigilance is a way of life to those committed to a joyful and fulfilling relationship with God. This is "drinking the cup" that He drank. This is "only doing what I see my Father in heaven doing." It is the way to the fullness of joy, fellowship, and purpose that you have prayed for, craved, and dreamed about.

Stuffing New Understanding into Old Doctrines

The ultimate goal in my sojourn through this life is not to make it easy on myself. My goal is to make it so that my Father can trust me and use me. I want the world to see Him through my actions, whether or not I ever open my mouth. My passion is to be as close to an exact representation of His Kingdom as I possibly can. Authenticity is the only thing that will cause the nations to run to Him. The world looks at Christianity in general and sees nothing that causes them to run to our light. Most believers blame the devil and anything else that comes to mind as to why this is so. There is something grossly missing in our faith experience, our faith expression, and our belief system when the nations run away from us, rather than to us. The Ancient prophets Micah and Isaiah saw the nations running *to* Him in reverence. But today, the nations do not even fear Him. Why is this so?

Why did the world love and run toward Mother Teresa but run away from the televangelist? Could it be an issue of authenticity? Authentic sons have nothing to hide and nothing to defend. They do not judge and they do not condemn. Through their own yieldedness to Him, they are living the Divine Life of our Elder Brother. They allow His love, compassion, and mercy to flow through them. They live in quiet attentiveness and prayer that they might see, hear and do what they see their own Father doing on this planet.

I refuse to blame anything or anyone else for the conditions of the society in which we life. The issue is not even the unregenerated heart of the world. Rather, it is the unsurrendered heart of the religious world that knows all the right words but does not have a clue as to Who our Father really is. To that end, by God's grace, I want my friendship with Him to be open and honest. I refuse to allow my actions to nullify what He is saying through me. It is my surrendered life that demonstrates the real Life of Jesus to those around me. My words mean nothing if they are not lived. If I am afraid of what I might hear from Him, then so be it. But I will not put on a show of piety for the sake of religious expediency. I AM A SON.

Folks love the verse about old and new wineskins when they talk about the things of the Spirit. But many do not realize that the verse is about establishing a principle of change. The principle is simply that new understanding cannot be put into existing doctrines or worldviews willy-nilly. This principle is not only addressing those who do not accept the things of the Spirit, but rather to all who have a resistance to change. We cannot pick and choose how to apply a principle to our lives any more than we can pick and choose how we will apply gravity. It is here in the crucible of humility that we discover that God does not bend to our will or our belief systems. We are beholden to Him and the way He has ordered the universe.

Sons Drink the Cup

We must remember that this book is about maturing sons, not meandering prodigals. I cannot build a fence around everything that sounds controversial. I am not writing to those who are content to stay where they are or to those looking for an excuse to go off in rebellion. I am looking for the desperate and the famished, those who live with focused determination in their sojourn with their King. I am not a pastor, and I will not coddle the vacillating or comfort the stubborn. This is not a "religiously correct" book. It is not for those who are too squeamish to look at things in a different light—for that is how real growth occurs.

Most of us have, quite unconsciously, determined what we believe, and nothing can change us. We have a doctrine of transformation but not the reality of transformation—for we are mostly unwilling to allow a different thought to challenge what we have always believed. We have a doctrine of being on a sojourn but have little idea how that is fleshed out in time and space. It is a startling fact—most of us have stopped learning, which means that we have stopped changing. And if we are not changing, we are not becoming more like Him. Oh, we love to learn about new Greek and Hebrew words. We love a new revelation. We love the banter of discussing the true meaning of a verse of Scripture, but it never crosses our mind that the *evidence* that we are on a journey is that things actually change. If I am really on a journey, I should be changing. I should be shedding more of myself and taking on more of Him. I should be decreasing in visible ways. My ways should be giving way to His will in a noticeable fashion. And at the very least, my transformation should be detectable to those closest to me. This is a major difference between religion and authentic relationship.

Karl Marx was right. Religion *is* the opiate of the people. It *does* lull the masses to sleep with a false sense of personal satisfaction and gratification, a false sense superiority. Religion satisfies the outward man with rituals, pre-texted prayers, rote memorization of denominational doctrines, and headquarter-approved Bible studies. Religion demands outward conformity but ignores the inner man. Yes, religion is the enemy of authentic union with God—the real union of life between God and man that He has always intended.

When dealing with the spirit of religion that has so many of our brothers and sisters bound, we are often too afraid of saying something that will offend—and so many of us say nothing at all. We are so concerned about discouraging the weak that we frustrate the strong. We try to placate the clueless while ignoring the hungry.

There are countless pastors whose goal is to keep the sheep happy so they keep coming, working, and tithing. There are numerous leaders who will dumb down the truth to fill their pews, who will coddle those who are not sure they are saved, who will feed the flock just enough to keep them alive but not enough to grow into their destiny. And worse, they don't really seem to care. I cannot tell you the number of leaders I have worked with, or tried to work with, over the years who simply have turned a calling into a career path, doing what is best for themselves. I have refused many who wanted to publish because I saw who and what they really were. To this day I cannot understand how these folks can sleep at night knowing what they are doing in ignoring the cries and needs of the people for the sake of their own gain.

All this is happening while those whose hearts are burning for Him are ignored or told they are too intense, overly zealous, insensitive to the weak, or perhaps even rebellious. The world will continue to fall to its chaotic death while we are learning new songs, paving new parking lots, and praying for each other. It reminds me of Nero playing his fiddle while Rome burns. It makes no sense to me at all.

But meanwhile, our King is on a search for sons who will pay the price, for those who will drink the cup and make a covenant with Him by sacrifice—their own sacrifice.

Questions for the Courageous

1. Have you ever experienced "new wine" from God? What changes to your "wineskin" did it bring about in your life and ministry?

2. Have you ever engaged in religious activity as a replacement for genuine relationship with your Father? What made you realize the difference?

3. Do you feel that there is a "cup" that He has set before you to drink? What is it? Are you ready to drink it?

Chapter 10

THE TELL-TALE DISCONNECT

> My dear son,
> You, like way too many incredibly gifted folks, have given up on destiny. But I have not. I still hold My dreams for you close to My heart! It's too easy to fall for the lies of those who do not understand mercy, cannot grasp hope, and will never understand My determined love for you that forgives again and again and again in full confidence that you will change. I AM leading your cheering section. After all, I know how I made you. I know what is inside of you! So no, I will never give up on you, and neither should you!

Behold, You desire truth in the inward parts, and in the hidden part You will make me to know wisdom.
—PSALM 51:6

Humanity's disconnect with reality has never been more glaring than it is in these opening years of the 21st century. Man lives in a delusional world of his own imagination, believing whatever he decides is correct with very little corroborating evidence. Consciously or unconsciously, we look for information that confirms our view of the world—including politics and religion—and rejects information that challenges it. It is quite ironic in light of this generation's claim that they need to see everything objectively verified by science before they believe. This disconnect is found securely lodged in most of humanity. The advent of social media has only exacerbated this problem.

Man wants to believe what is most convenient, most entertaining, least demanding, and most easily attainable. Those most likely to "remain in the Wilderness" are those who are best at holding on to a belief that makes personal change unnecessary. These are the ones who want the most and yet are the most unwilling to pay the price to attain it. Thinking that fulfillment is the result of gathering things, these tend to fill their lives with temporal objects and experiences and yet wonder why they still feel so empty and directionless. Let's face it, we have all been there. This way of thinking will keep most of us far from our potential and the fulfillment we want.

Those who call themselves Christians should be the shining masters of authentic reality and hope. We should be the group that least fears the inevitability of life's worst times. We, above all, should have experienced the saving grace of Christ both for this life and the next, understanding and living the indefinable glory of surrendered living. As yielded disciples we have the distinct advantage of demonstrating what life can be when one determines to live in synchronized harmony with the One who holds reality in the palm of His hand.

Living out of the midst of this heavenly reality does not mean everything in life will be perfect. It does mean, however, that everything in life has purpose and meaning even when things are going badly. Maturing sons hold to the truth that all things work together for good because they are orchestrated from their Father. These sons know by experience that their Father always has their best interests at the heart of His dealings with them. They know life is not like a rudderless ship in an open sea. We are neither here by accident, nor do we walk alone on this sojourn through life. The dream that our Father has dreamed for each was at the forefront of His thoughts when He lovingly and purposefully wove us together in our mother's womb. There, with our personal destiny in mind as His driving force, He made us with everything we would need to fulfill it. Our confidence is that the circumstances of life will bring our destiny to the forefront of fulfillment so that our contribution to the planet may be made to its fullest intention. This is our peace and, most certainly, this is our rest. Unfortunately, however, many believers are as disconnected from their King as everyone else in the world. Few of us have come to understand that our faith is far more than a confession. Rather, our faith is rooted in experience born of actual interaction with the Divine. This conscious interaction keeps us connected both to Him and to reality—life as it really is.

No Earthly Good

Back in the early days of charismania, there was a saying that reflected the lifestyles of too many folks: "That person is so heavenly minded that they are no earthly good." What this actually meant was that some folks were apparently so "connected" with the Spirit that they were no good for anything. Their spiritual maturity came to be measured solely by their ability to "move in the Spirit" or function in one of the gifts of the Spirit. But in the meantime, they were not reliable and their pursuit of "spirit" replaced their love for humanity.

Soon, many charismatic believers began to deny their sickness, their pain, and their difficult circumstances. In an attempt to prove that they had bold faith, they also denied that they had any needs! They seemed to forget that a miracle only occurs where there is a need for one, where there is a lack of some kind, where something is broken. In reality, we experience the miracle-working power of God when we are able to first recognize that we have a problem. It is only then that we can believe God to overcome it. Hence, the false premise that we should deny the brokenness of our humanity with its sickness and disease added to the disconnect between the natural and the spiritual. For many Charismatic believers, this led to a lifestyle that was fanciful, untethered to reality, and spiritually unfruitful.

Staying in touch with reality is the best way to experience the fullness of all God has for us. Remember, Abraham did not grow strong in faith by *ignoring* the deadness of Sarah's womb or the weakness of his own body. Rather, he contemplated it honestly and soberly. He grew strong even as he saw the barrenness of her womb and gave glory to God.

> *In hope against hope he* [Abraham] *believed.... Without becoming weak in faith he contemplated his own body, now as good as dead since he was about a hundred years old, and the deadness of Sarah's womb; yet, with respect to the promise of God, he did not waver in unbelief but grew strong in faith, giving glory to God, and being fully assured that what God had promised, He was able also to perform* (Romans 4:18-21 NASB).

Our Elder Brother was far more heavenly minded than anyone who ever lived, and yet He was also the most earthly good of anyone who ever walked on this planet. He saw the intense need of the people and ministered to them. He focused on the ones the religious leaders of the day ignored. He gave Himself to the most vulnerable and the most at risk. His love and compassion for the needy gave His message wings and validated Who He is. His mercy opened the hearts of the generations that would come long after He left this realm. Thus His influence and ministry has endured and will continue to endure for all the ages.

But He, because He continues forever, has an unchangeable priesthood. Therefore He is also able to save to the uttermost those who come to God through Him, since He always lives to make intercession for them (Hebrews 7:24-25).

The Now: Where Miracles Happen

Now faith is the substance of things hoped for, the evidence of things not seen (Hebrews 11:1).

Some of you will remember Oral Roberts and his powerful life message on living in the "now." He saw something that too many just ignore—that a major key to maturity is the ability to live in the "now," in the reality of life, consciously connected with the issues in this dimension. Miracles occur in the honest reality of the moment; that is in the "now."

Those who can admit where they are, what sickness afflicts them, what temptation overcomes them (without shifting blame to some other person or event) are the ones ripe for Divine intervention. Repentance is not just a "get out of jail free" card. Rather, it is a solemn confession of sin coupled with a determination to surrender to the change that only Jesus can accomplish. It is acknowledging the place of need that allows the Lord to minister His deliverance to us. In His generous Kingdom, it is only self-sufficiency or a lack of faith that shuts Him out. It is sobering indeed to remember that Jesus said, "It is not those who are healthy who need a physician, but those who are sick" (Matt. 9:12 NASB).

Eliminating the disconnect between myself and the world around me begins within my own heart and life. God wants truth in the "inward parts." As painful as it can be at times, being truthful in the innermost part of us is the primary key to understanding the struggle of those around us. It releases the love and compassion of God through us like little else can.

The crucible of everyday life should keep us in touch with the sufferings of others while we, ourselves, suffer. To say or otherwise believe that we should not suffer is to make one greater than the King, Who Himself had to suffer to learn obedience, to be able to minister effectively to mankind.

> *He had to be made like His brethren in all things, so that He might become a merciful and faithful high priest in things pertaining to God, to make propitiation for the sins of the people. For since He Himself was tempted in that which He has suffered, He is able to come to the aid of those who are tempted* (Hebrews 2:17-18 NASB).

The Ancients' Reality Check

Contrary to the way that some "enlightened" ones teach today, our growth, strength, success, and fulfillment are the result of *facing* the difficulties of life, not ignoring them. I cannot reckon myself smart; I must study. I cannot reckon my bills paid; I must work, save, budget, and pay them.

The Ancients did not just "reckon" themselves out of Egypt; they had to actually pack their stuff, risk their lives, and flee their oppressors. Jesus did not just "reckon" Himself dead on the Cross; He had to actually give Himself to be the real flesh and blood sacrifice that would free humanity of their bondage. Likewise, we do not merely "reckon ourselves dead" as an exercise of religious reprogramming. This kind of intellectual gymnastics may soothe the mind but does nothing to bring peace to the soul or hope to the heart. Rather, it adds to the sense of disconnection that keeps our heart broken and our vision dull.

It is not for man to rewrite the laws of nature, either in this dimension or the dimension of Spirit. Man must see the reality as things are and then we will understand the incredible nature of the miraculous. Rather than ignoring it, Abraham "looked intently at the deadness of Sarah's womb" (see Rom. 4:19). He was not afraid to contemplate the obstacle that would prevent God's will from being done. He did not ignore the problem; rather, he stared right at it. And while fully acknowledging the deadness of Sarah's womb and his own great age, Abraham still believed that God would do what He had said He would do. Thus he "grew strong in faith as He gave glory to God."

Faith versus Fantasy

The faith that is based on a clear word from God is very different from wishful thinking. Just because I say something is so does not make it so. I can decide gravity is just my imagination, but when I drop a glass out of my hand it is still going to crash on the floor. I do not *think* my way to a miracle. Rather, I admit the problem, but I do not waver in unbelief, knowing that if God wills, I will see change. I do not ignore the laws of nature; I simply believe that God is greater than them. Rather than minimizing the circumstances, I magnify the King Who is greater than the need.

Man cannot expect that nature will bend to the whims of mere mortal thought. It is foolish to expect that God Himself will obligingly redesign His plan to match the personal opinions of an individual. Such beliefs are convenient, to be sure, but they are not intellectually honest and certainly not faithfully applied. Authentic sons speak only what the King has already decreed—nothing more and nothing less.

The Plumb Line of True Identity

The spirit of William Ernest Henley lives on in the rebellious nature of most of humanity. His declaration made him famous before man but did little to impress God. Henley concludes his poem "Invictus" quite famously with, "I am the master of my fate, I am the captain of my soul." Somehow, I suspect that there was no Divine nervousness when those words first went into the heavens and neither was there was an earthy shudder when he spoke them across the land. Man's words, declared in his own strength, do not obligate God to do anything.

Not knowing who we really are opens up a Pandora's box filled with various ideologies, religions, and cultural standards all vying for attention. When there is no established inner heart marker that defines who we are, there is no plumb line. Where there is no plumb line, there is no rule of society, no order to existence among civilized peoples. But even nature itself has a definable order to it that, if ignored, will cause a breakdown in whatever ecosystem the breach has occurred. We are seeing these ecological breakdowns happen across the earth. Nature demands order for growth and development to continue to its highest form of expression and life. A mere intellectual change in thought about natural order does not change the predetermined laws of nature. The laws of nature will continue to humble us until we learn to live differently. So thinking differently alone changes nothing unless it is nurtured by faith that is proven by actions that complement our faith.

Of course, it is the arrogance of man that makes him think that as he believes, so goes the universe. In his own self-inflated view of himself, he tends to believe that the universe is beholden to his way of thinking, that he can decree a thing and it will be as he has randomly determined that it should be. Whether that decree is natural or spiritual, man's misplaced confidence in his own words is remarkable. Without real proof, we continue to believe that the spoken words of a man change everything. Our words do have power, it is true, but if a miracle does happen to occur with a decree, it is only because the King has already ordered it.

The Tell-Tale Disconnect

Instead of playing the games that amount to nothing more than humanism with a spiritual veneer over it, sons should arise into their true sonship by declaring with the Firstborn, "I only do what I see my Father in heaven doing."

In spite of our immaturity and presumption, the truth remains that man's response to God *will* change everything. When Jesus taught us to pray, "Thy Kingdom come, Thy will be done on *earth* as it is in heaven," He laid down the pattern of redemption's plan for all things spiritual and all things natural. Understanding this simple principle keeps our spiritual ears attentive to the Voice of God and keeps our feet firmly planted on the ground. Staying in union with God makes us those through whom He will bring His ultimate plan into fruition. A humble acknowledgement of our sonship keeps us ready to do the bidding of the King, for the sake of all creation. For truly, our destiny is wrapped up in the destiny of all things, and all creation is waiting and groaning for this moment. Let the sons arise!

Questions for the Desperate

1. Can you remember a time when you made a presumptuous decree or prayer? What was the result?

2. Have you, like Abraham, ever been able to contemplate the hopelessness of a situation and yet still believe God for a promised fulfillment? Have you seen the answer come to pass yet, or are you still waiting?

3. If sons only speak what they hear their Father saying, have you heard God say anything concerning some of the most vexing problems in your life and in this world? What did He say about it?

4. Again, if sons only speak what they hear their Father saying, does it give you pause when you are about to speak in the Name of Lord? Does this knowledge make you more cautious?

Chapter 11

SO THIS IS WHO I AM

> My dear son,
> So this is who you truly are. Awesome, isn't it? Man did not make you a son. I did. The Divine DNA you carry has destiny you are just beginning to discover. The churning in your heart is Me, your cheering section. Yes, I am praying for you, drawing you, speaking to you. Today, as you hear My Voice, listen and follow. Your life will never be as it was. Let's do this together. I have My full confidence in you.

The son of Seth, the son of Adam, the son of God.
—LUKE 3:38 NASB.

For you are all sons of God through faith in Christ Jesus.
—GALATIANS 3:26 NASB

My Father is Divine in nature. His offspring—you and I—are the same. There is something very different about those who carry the essence of two dimensions, both natural and spiritual, within them. These are the people spoken of in the Scriptures of whom "the world is not worthy."

Within every human being abides the portal to the realm of the heavenlies. We are the gateway to two very different worlds that have little in common with each other. On one side is the very human, very earthy side that naturally wants to live in the fulfillment of our human cravings. The other side is the spiritual, other-dimensional realm where we live by feelings from that dimension, thus abandoning the natural dimension to become totally otherworldly in action and attitude.

There seems to be the inexplicable need to either be all spirit, ignoring the human realm, or to be all natural, ignoring the spiritual realm. But we are neither wholly natural nor wholly spiritual. We are something brand-new in the universe, and we are a force to be reckoned with when we begin to have even an inkling of who we really are. We must explore, discover, and walk in this new reality with sober-minded determination, allowing truth to invade all our most sacred and secure thoughts. This is how we shall become the embodiment of our King with His attributes, love, and predetermined plan. His will, His way, and His ultimate intention must prevail through man if the rest of humanity is to see Him for who He truly is. Therefore, I must allow Him to increase, as I decrease.

Here Come the Sons of God

To that end, the dimension of Spirit must be studied and understood in order for us to adequately and successfully be able to navigate it. Conversely, all that is born of Spirit must experience the full measure of time and space to successfully understand the plight of those naturally anchored in dust. But the two become One in Christ. All-God and all-man must come together to make a new species, a new life that has never before been seen either in this realm or the realm of Spirit. This union, determined by God from before time began, will bring about eternal redemption on both sides of the celestial shore.

For here, in this new creation, man is no longer alone. God is no longer alone. Something never before seen is blossoming. Something that has never entered the imagination of man is taking place before the very eyes of the universe. Everything is changing. Everything is taking on new meaning, new hope, new possibilities, and, of course, new love. God has bent Himself down to the lower-than-the-angels life form called humanity. He has entrusted Himself to mere humans, who are now the resting place of the Divine. The "new creation man" has denied himself, turned from complete dependence on earthy ways of mere existence, and renounced his trust in a world where fallen logic confines and controls thought and destiny. Here, at the place of Divine humility and human response, something eternally new is taking shape. Sons are searching out their Father. They are shedding the restrictions of mere humanity to become part of a multidimensional carrier of all things Divine and all things natural. This one New Man, this new creation, this never-before-seen species is emerging to rule with Him, with He who shares His Divinity with former mere mortals—you and I.

The Religious Have Fallen

And when the people of Ashdod arose early in the morning, there was Dagon, fallen on its face to the earth before the ark of the Lord (1 Samuel 5:3).

The idol Dagon, the Philistine "father of Baal," is losing his grip on the souls of men. Nature groans in its newly realized hope, waiting for sons of God to show themselves worthy, equipped, and capable of carrying the mantle of sons. The old definitions will no longer work. The failed religious ways of thinking must give way to the realities that the Ancients saw when they prophesied the union of man and God so long ago. The time has come upon us. Eternity is breaking into time and space. The time is now, as it has been since Jesus walked out of the tomb. Here come the sons of God.

I AM a person who is 100 percent man and filled with a Sprit who is 100 percent God. But what I AM means nothing if I do not give way to the work of the Divine, my Father, within my being. His Life is rising within that He might make us more than we have ever dreamed possible. He has made Himself detectable, approachable, and reachable to a dimensional being far lower than Himself. Such knowledge is too great for us; it is nearly impossible to understand with our natural limitations. Nonetheless, those who will dare see this have stepped out of the obscurity of gray lines and uncertain images. We can now see as we are seen. We can know as we are known. When we dare to venture beyond the accepted boundaries, the conventional norms of mediocrity, we will move as few have moved and see what few have seen. We will live as only One has lived, for we will become what we behold.

I AM a son, and I am far more than this finite mind has imagined or even hoped for. But if I AM wise, I will never allow the limitations of man or his religion, science, or philosophies keep me from experiencing what my Father is to me right now in this present moment. But what I choose to follow will be who I become—either a God/man who functions from the mind of the Almighty or a mere man who functions out of the need-centered passions of a mortal.

The mind of the Almighty at work in this God/man is focused on lifting all men from the mediocrity of the earthy to the unparalleled wonders of the union of God and man. This Divine work puts the needs of the vulnerable before my own—as if I need anything in this multidimensional reality that is now my way of life. Thinking as a mere mortal is now foreign to me, as the fullness of Him expresses Himself in and through me and satisfies my soul. Yes, even in my weakness. Maturing sons grow in their ability to rest in the Almighty instead of themselves. They recognize their own self-centered, self-gratifying, self-indulgent thoughts and run from their power and influence for they are the last remaining hindrance of the expression of the Divine within.

Maturing sons allow nothing of this world to divide their allegiance to one another—not politics, not denomination, and not sports. We should be as single-focused as Jesus was when He walked the earth. The more we recognize the intention of our King, the more we will be committed to the expression of the King to the seeking and troubled hearts. We will become a servant to all peoples, doing all we can to afford everyone the best opportunity to find Him, yielding to His ultimate intention for them.

Maturing sons want nothing less than union with their Creator. They long to be lost in the Divine where all things natural are illumined by a love that transforms everything. Their example to others makes them the salt of the earth to all men.

Hush, God's Talking

I have no intention of being satisfied with less than He has wrought for me when He rose from the grave. I refuse to limit His Life within. I will not allow my finite brain, my mortal understanding of Spirit, my doctrinal, cultural, or political bias to sidetrack me from the fullness of His expression to me, in me, and through me. In truth, I can say before God that anything I think, believe, or have experienced—anything I have been taught or that I have taught others that is contrary to the thoughts of My Father as He truly is—has no place in me. Those things that subconsciously sidetrack my union with my Father, whom I cherish above all else on this planet or in any other dimension, must have absolutely no place in my life. My daily meditations help me to see these places. But make no mistake, corrections to deeply held beliefs are not always easy to hear or accept. Even so, we grow in the Divine nature as we hear and respond to these uncomfortable things from our Father.

This Is a Journey

In the unbridled enthusiasm of the moment when we see something new along the road of life, it is easy to forget that we are on a journey and camp at our new discovery. But God is taking us on a path not paved by man. No matter how wonderful the sites are along the way, no matter the power of what we have newly discovered, there is always more that is still ahead of us. We must keep moving forward toward the upward call of God in Christ, for whom many have suffered the loss of all things, even their own lives. When I think about this holy cloud of witnesses, I cannot allow myself to camp anywhere along the way. For their sake as well as my own, I must go on.

Of course, we never forget the glory of what we have seen. Rather, what we have learned must become an integral part of who we are now. My early encounters will forever be a part of who I AM. They will forever change the way I live, what I believe, and how I treat others. But there are many encounters. There is so much more to what I AM and the dream God has for me. In my heart, I am not interested in only an occasional encounter, as though He comes and goes. I am not satisfied with momentary visitations, words, prophecies, healing, or visions of glory. The empowering Christ of God dwells within. My entire life is an intimate interaction between the King and me. I AM in union with my Father!

Jesus is not a signs-and-wonders-driven Pentecostal person and neither am I. I am not camping at that experience, as wonderful as it was. If a "greater than Solomon is here" then certainly a greater than Pentecost is here. I am no more settling in Pentecost than the Ancients should have settled in the Wilderness. All of these "signs and wonders" are things that flow out of His compassion:

And when Jesus went out He saw a great multitude; and He was moved with compassion for them, and healed their sick (Matthew 14:14).

The attributes of my King are inner strength, emotional stability, and spiritual illumination. He was "moved with compassion" for us and still is. Everything eternal flowing out of the Son is released into time and space by the sheer force of Divine passion and unmitigated love. This love flows from the depths of our Father; through us, His sons; and out to the rest of creation, our fellow human beings.

Truly Quantum Leaps

Like me, eternity is in breathless anticipation. The earth groans in travail, waiting for sons to appear on the scene. The appearance of the sons will initiate quantum leaps into things unimaginable, things never seen before on earth. Sons are not merely moved from one side of the Wilderness to the other but are making truly life-altering leaps into the very heart of God. They are not recognized as Pentecostal, Charismatic, or any other religious experience, denominational, organizational, secular, or governmental organization.

They are the ones through whom Jesus Himself will be poured upon the earth. These are men and women who are not distracted by the shiny things along the way, especially the religious and political shiny things. These folks are not so easily flattered by mere mortal man and they refuse to be sidetracked. Like their Elder Brother, they are on a mission. Like Jesus, who "set His face like flint" toward Jerusalem, they are not turned aside to fame, influence, or money. Like Jesus, they are only impassioned with seeing what their Father is doing, no matter what else is going on around them. They have crossed the Jordan. They have paid the price, quite literally unto death, to see His will done on this planet. They are the maturing sons of God.

We Have Not Been This Way Before

No, we have not been this way before, but Isaiah has. His vision of this company of maturing sons is the beat of my heart, the desire of my life. But I also realize that the best way to get there is to become what I see, what I believe, what I pray for.

Isaiah saw those who would encourage one another, not compete against one another. He saw sons strengthening one another, not taking advantage of the weak. He saw a company of maturing sons, mighty but compassionate, overcoming but humble in every respect, who were secure in who they are, who have made a covenant with the King by sacrifice—their own.

He Saw Restored Sons

> *O afflicted one, storm-tossed, and not comforted, behold, I will set your stones in antimony, and your foundations I will lay in sapphires. Moreover, I will make your battlements of rubies, and your gates of crystal, and your entire wall of precious stones* (Isaiah 54:11-12 NASB).

> *Then the eyes of the blind will be opened and the ears of the deaf will be unstopped. Then the lame will leap like a deer, and the tongue of the mute will shout for joy. For waters will break forth in the wilderness and streams in the Arabah* (Isaiah 35:5-6 NASB).

He Saw Ministering Sons

> *Say to those with anxious heart, "Take courage, fear not. Behold, your God will come with vengeance; the recompense of God will come, but He will save you." Then the eyes of the blind will be opened and the ears of the deaf will*

be unstopped. Then the lame will leap like a deer, and the tongue of the mute will shout for joy (Isaiah 35:4-6 NASB).

He Saw Holy, Overcoming Sons

A highway will be there, a roadway, and it will be called the Highway of Holiness. The unclean will not travel on it, but it will be for him who walks that way, and fools will not wander on it. No lion will be there, nor will any vicious beast go up on it; these will not be found there. But the redeemed will walk there (Isaiah 35:8-9 NASB).

He Saw Victorious Sons

And the ransomed of the Lord will return and come with joyful shouting to Zion, with everlasting joy upon their heads. They will find gladness and joy, and sorrow and sighing will flee away (Isaiah 35:10 NASB).

Even King David saw into this generation when he said, "As for the saints who are in the earth, they are the majestic ones in whom is all my delight" (Ps. 16:3 NASB); and again, "How lovely are Your dwelling places, O Lord of hosts!" (Ps. 84:1 NASB). Micah also wrote what he saw as he peered through the ages:

"In that day," declares the Lord, "I will assemble the lame and gather the outcasts, even those whom I have afflicted. I will make the lame a remnant and the outcasts a strong nation, and the Lord will reign over them in Mount Zion from now on and forever. As for you, tower of the flock, Hill of the daughter of Zion, to you it will come—even the former dominion will come, the kingdom of the daughter of Jerusalem" (Micah 4:6-8 NASB).

No, it is true, we have not been there, but we have the records of those who have been there through their prophetic eyes. The things they tell us cause me to leap within with the expectation that what they saw could be this generation.

"He's My Dad"

"He's my dad," said my son to that author so many years ago. "I do whatever he wants me to do." This simple yet profound discovery changes the course of human history, beginning with mine and yours. But I know you. You have read this book this far. Your heart must be burning up by now as the Spirit of your Father embraces you within, convincing you that you are, in fact, His son.

Questions for Focused Sons

1. In what way(s) are you limiting the Holy One within you? What do you feel your Father saying to you in response to that?

2. Are you becoming aware of your own Wilderness experience and lifestyle? Does the thought of leaving the comfort of the Wilderness and facing the new challenges of the Promised Land scare or intimidate you? If so, how are you facing these fears?

3. How different would the world look if there were many sons who looked just like Jesus walking around? Can you see your calling and placement among these sons? Why did you answer that question as you did?

Chapter 12

JESUS: THE PATTERN SON

My dear son,
Once you have seen the glory of God within your heart, there is no going back. I am not talking about the outward parlor tricks of the flamboyant; I am talking about the deep, inner reality of union with your King. This reality cannot be faked. This cannot be imitated. For when you truly see Him, you are transformed into His image. People see Him and not so much you. Either He flows effortlessly, powerfully, with passionate determination and Life, or He does not. Everyone will see the difference between the authentic and the not-so-authentic. But be at peace. You are yielding. You are changing. You are becoming the image of the One you have devoted your life to. I have every confidence in you. I know your heart. It is just like Mine.

The Pattern Forerunner

There was never a person like Jesus on this planet. There was never One who lived like Him or died like Him—enveloped with purpose, empowered by destiny, and motivated by Divine love. There was never One who came like Him, with specific purpose to present Himself as the sinless Offering so that all peoples, throughout all time, would have personal access to their Creator.

He brought a new picture of the Divine to the planet as His life was lived in sharp contrast to those who said they knew God and tasked themselves with leading the people to Him.

The religious leaders of the day lived in opulence while He lived in poverty. They dressed in the best the world could provide while He dressed as a peasant. They lived in magnificent homes while the Son of Man had no place to lay His head. The leaders of the day were served by the lowly while Jesus was a servant to all, especially the lowly. They commanded the attention of the elite while Jesus drew the attention of the broken, the hopeless, the sinner, the sick, and the needy. The religious leaders catered to the rich while Jesus brought hope to the poor. The leaders waited for the folks to come to them in the temples, while Jesus went out to the people on hillsides, the seashore, and in their own homes. The leaders were at the top of the religious food chain, but Jesus gave Himself as bread and wine to feed our hungry souls. He went to the masses even as the religious gatekeepers of the day closed their doors—not only to the masses, but also to the Son of God Himself.

The Pattern Son

Seeing the pattern of the Son of God is eternal as it is practical. It is deliberate as it is empowering. It is a pattern recognizable by those through whom He lives. But these understand that Jesus is far more than a pattern, as though we merely copy His methods and repeat His words. Jesus can do His own work, build His own Church, and rule His own Kingdom. He only needs us to surrender to Him that He might do His Divine purposes through us. As Jesus emptied Himself, so must we empty ourselves of all things fleshy that obscure His beautiful image in us. When we see the attributes of our Elder Brother coming through our lives, we know the Pattern Son is building His Kingdom within our hearts.

> *For whom He foreknew, He also predestined to be conformed to the image of His Son, that He might be the firstborn among many brethren* (Romans 8:29).

For some, Jesus is the Savior. To others, He has also become the Pattern. But for some, He has become King. Their heart is His Kingdom, and His Life shines through them like the beacon of hope that He truly is. We must move from Jesus as merely a pattern to the ultimate of God's intention and desire—union with His creation.

The Recognizable Son

> *For you know the grace of our Lord Jesus Christ, that though He was rich, yet for your sakes He became poor, that you through His poverty might become rich* (2 Corinthians 8:9).

Jesus was never really difficult to find. You knew where He was by the masses who followed Him wherever He went. His love for the people was unmistakable. He served them morning and night. He walked with them, among them, although He was the Son of God. But that is the point. The more you know who you are, the more you are not afraid to be a servant to all men. For you have discovered who you are; serving even in the smallest task does not change who you are. One does not sacrifice his place by serving mankind. He can only enhance it, although that is the last reason for being an authentic servant.

The greatness of our King was evident by the way He never enforced His position, never intimidated the people, never belittled them or forced them to serve Him. His greatness was proven again and again by His humility, His softness of heart, and compassion. He made the Divine not only tangible to the masses but approachable to the lowly, poor, and forgotten.

Probably the greatest evidence that a person knows who they are is that they are not afraid that they will lose their identity by serving those in desperate need. They do not lord their position over those they "serve" because they know that Divine reality cannot be forced on anyone. The gifts and promises of God are not bestowed upon a person by demands or intimidation. The sons of God know that these things grow naturally in our lives as we give ourselves to Him like the soil gives itself to a seed.

Everything that is held in the Father is released to a willing humanity by Divine love, first exampled in our Elder Brother, Jesus Christ, and still exampled in Him through the likes of simple folks like you and I. The evidence of Divine love is bestowed upon us through the working of that same love first in us, because of the death and Resurrection of Jesus, and then through us because of our daily death to ourselves.

The first-century believers were recognized by the love they had one for another. It is significant that they were not first tagged for their miracles, their general charismatica, or any other earthy evidence. They were labeled as Christians because of the love they had for one another. So it should be with us.

Fleshy attempts to go anywhere He has not prepared will undoubtedly result in frustration. Many gatekeepers of religion will never open the doors to authentic sons any more than they did to the authentic Christ. It is for this reason that Jesus went to the masses. If we want to be as effective as Jesus was and still is, we also must go to the masses rather than the "top." We should not expect the religious hierarchy to open the doors for us or to seek to climb to the top of the religious empires ourselves.

> *Therefore Jesus also, that He might sanctify the people with His own blood, suffered outside the gate. Therefore let us go forth to Him, outside the camp, bearing His reproach* (Hebrews 13:12-13).

It is in the place of "outside the camp," where the King opens the doors and gives favor to those who carry the Divine and all that it represents.

The Forgiving Son

I have been amazed at how quickly Jesus forgave the sinner. It rankles my religious thought to think that Jesus forgave the woman caught in adultery before she even asked for it. It turns my doctrine on its side to think that Jesus forgave Peter after he denied Him the night before He was sacrificed. He called every one of His disciples out of the lifestyle they lived in without a verbal commitment or promise from them to stick with Him. He didn't first tell them to change, clean up their way of life, or follow a set of rules in order to be His followers, let alone His personal disciples. He had something that we have not yet really comprehended.

But then, I am thinking like a typical pastor or religious minister. For we have formulated a set of responses, an initiation of sorts, that one must go through in order to be accepted into the flock of the Redeemed. Until these are met, one will always be an outsider, a little less than the rest of the group.

But it was not so with Jesus. When He spoke, He did not build walls of separation between Himself and those to whom He spoke. He talked to their hearts. He stirred their spirits and gave them hope. Even the officers sent by the Pharisees to arrest Jesus found that they could not do it. The report was amazing: "Never has a man spoken the way this man speaks" (John 7:46 NASB).

The Gathering Son

Jesus was the consummate gatherer. He was driven by one rule: "love them all." He knew the power of the love that He embodied and He trusted that love to transform those who were touched by Him. Those who were offended with Him were offended at His love, at His willingness to gather the tax collector, the prostitute, the adulterer, the sinner. He sat with them where they were sitting, ate what they were eating, and talked to them without condescending words.

Amazingly enough, this Christ of God—this Son, our Elder Brother who was with God, in God from before the beginning of time—would continue His work of loving, gathering, and transforming those who are willing to allow Him to live His religion-free Life through them. While not accepting the enslaving sin that binds us, He knew the way to our freedom begins by giving us a taste of what true love really is.

This is the same love that bound our Creator Father to our Redeemer Son from eternity past, and through which all creation is established. "If you had known Me, you would have known My Father also; and from now on you know Him and have seen Him" (John 14:7).

The pattern of this gathering, redeeming Son cannot be clearer. Love is the foundation, the building blocks, the building, and the contents of the House. Anything less is not the exact representation of Who He really is—both Father and Son.

The Pattern Light of the World

Then Jesus spoke to them again, saying, "I am the light of the world. He who follows Me shall not walk in darkness, but have the light of life" (John 8:12).

The Light of the world came to this world, but we did not want Him. We murdered Him, not understanding that He was the Sacrifice Who would open the doors for billions of people throughout the ages to carry this eternal Light to the nations.

Maturing sons are conduits through whom the eternal Light of our Father shines, even as Jesus was the first Son through whom this eternal Light was visible in time and space. This is the Light the world longs to see. It is not the light of empty religious activity, not the light of human illumination, and not even the light of contemporary revival. It is simply the "light of life." The pattern is simple—we yield to the eternal Light that shone long before time began and thus we begin to shine ourselves. We are His "light show" to the world, showing His Life to anyone who will surrender to it. The more we respond to the Light, the brighter it will shine through us. The brighter it shines, the more clearly the contrast becomes between what is of God and what is not. It is this contrast that brings an individual to the point of decision. This Light shines in the heart of every man so that he can see for himself what is in him. The man then either surrenders to Him or runs away.

A surrendered life shines like a city on a hill. It serves those in need with a depth of selflessness that causes the Light of the King to radiate from them. The sons know that love itself is strong enough to draw humanity to eternity's Light. The sons who yield their lives in this way are ones through whom the world can see Him and His eternity. Their surrender fulfills Jesus' words to "let your light shine before men in such a way that they may see your good works, and glorify your Father who is in heaven" (Matt. 5:16 NASB).

The Pattern Sacrifice

That I may know Him and the power of His resurrection, and the fellowship of His sufferings, being conformed to His death, if, by any means, I may attain to the resurrection from the dead (Philippians 3:10-11).

When some resist this Light, the conflict begins between Light and the forces of darkness. Darkness has only one way to be free from the power of this compelling Light—it must eliminate it. And so, the Lamb of God was sacrificed. He was our example. Those who lead Light-filled lives in Christ will suffer persecution; some will even suffer death. But every time the darkness tries to snuff out a person who is a lamp of the Anointed of God, it only causes the Light of eternity to shine more brightly through others.

The determined goal of every maturing son is to remain a lamp through whom the Light of eternity may continuously shine. It is too easy to resort to human, worldly tactics to try to convince the world of the light we say we have. But maturing sons will not yield to any human, worldly, political, or fleshy methods. Their struggle is to allow only the Divine Light to do the convincing, the convicting, the calling to repentance, the transforming.

If anyone does not stumble in word, he is a perfect man, able also to bridle the whole body (James 3:2).

If we are determined to be the exact representation of His nature, then we must weigh carefully the words that flow from our mouths, the judgments that flow from our hearts, and the thoughts that fill our minds. No wonder we are admonished to put on the Mind of Christ.

We are encouraged that "whatever is true, whatever is honorable, whatever is right, whatever is pure, whatever is lovely, whatever is of good repute, if there is any excellence and if anything worthy of praise, dwell on these things." (Phil. 4:8 NASB) and, "Therefore if you have been raised up with Christ, keep seeking the things above, where Christ is, seated at the right hand of God. Set your mind on the things above, not on the things that are on earth. For you have died and your life is hidden with Christ in God" (Col. 3:1-3 NASB).

Maturing sons speak circumspectly, examining everything they say and think against the Spirit of Him Who must reign within us. A son knows that his opinion is never the point. This is part of his sacrifice. A son yields his opinions to the ways of our Father, which is always paramount in any situation. If I cannot yield my tongue, if I cannot yield my will to His in an argument, how will I ever yield my life? He is the Pattern Sacrifice we should be following. Our lifestyle is the sacrifice of our human rights to His eternal being, even as Jesus sacrificed His rights to His Father.

The Covenant Son

Till we all come to the unity of the faith and of the knowledge of the Son of God, to a perfect man, to the measure of the stature of the fullness of Christ; that we should no longer be children, tossed to and fro and carried about with every wind of doctrine, by the trickery of men, in the cunning craftiness of deceitful plotting (Ephesians 4:13-14).

Maturing sons have yielded to the love, teaching, and discipline of their Father. They have learned to willingly put His will above their own. They have relinquished their own rights in lieu of His purpose. They have heard and responded to the call of the Father as "He summons the heavens above, and the earth, to judge His people:

'Gather My godly ones to Me, those who have made a covenant with Me by sacrifice'" (Ps. 50:4-5 NASB).

Who is it the Father will trust in the days to come? Will it be the prodigals who will judge with Him? Will it be the angels? No and no. Such judgment is reserved for His maturing sons, the godly ones who have paid the price and have submitted to the transformational work of the King within them. These ones have taken no shortcuts, demanded no special treatment, and made no bargains with God. They give, serve, and sacrifice because they understand that they are the tithe of the Lord to the earth itself. They are the ones whom the Father has assigned to be the living proof on the planet that He is truly alive and well and living His life through once mere human beings. They are the evidence that all He has said is true.

They have proven to a skeptical humanity that He shows no partiality, no favoritism, and no free rides. Maturing sons, paying the price of obedience, inherit the promises of God. For they, more than any other, have allowed the King, the Christ of God, the Firstborn Son to shine more authentically through them with lessening resistance and little desire to adhere to their own prejudice, their own pride, their own need to be seen. This place is not reserved for a chosen few, however. It is for all who cut covenant with Him through their own sacrifice. All that God intends for humanity is available to all.

These sons give themselves willingly without considering how they would benefit, but that is to be expected. The thought of such bargaining with their Father is anathema to them. Their single desire is to be pleasing to Him, giving them joy, deep satisfaction, and inner tranquility. The sheer joy of giving is their motivation to give, and they have learned to give cheerfully. The sheer honor of serving the Father, the gratification of being a part of Him Who reigns in the heart is far greater than any earthy accolade, any earthy satisfaction or payoff.

The First Begotten

And He is the head of the body, the church, who is the beginning, the firstborn from the dead, that in all things He may have the preeminence (Colossians 1:18).

He is the Firstborn Son. He did not wait for the world to come to Him. From the very beginning, He was and still is the first to trust His Father with His very Life. He was the first to love unconditionally. The first to give without any thought of payback. The first to sit with the worst of sinners. The first to forgive those whose sin had overcome them. He was the first to embrace those who the elite would call the dregs of society. He was the first to love those who hated Him, the first to die that others might live. He was the first to die for even those who hate him. He is the first Covenant Pattern Son, the One Who lives through us.

As we surrender to His life within, we also will walk the earth bearing the Life Force of the Divine Himself. We become the ones who will convince the world that He is truly all He has said about Himself. We will be, like Him, the first to love; the first to forgive; the first to gather, to heal, to bless. We will be first to offer a smile, a word of hope, a hand to help. We will be first to show compassion, the first to encourage when there is no indication that any of it would be returned.

The maturing son rests in his Elder Brother. He knows that his life is the expression of the King on this planet. To that end, he submits His soul to Him who has transferred us from the kingdom of darkness to the Kingdom of His Beloved Son.

In this way, the maturing son also becomes a pattern son, allowing His Father to freely shine His Life through him. This is why Paul could say, "Imitate me, just as I also imitate Christ" (1 Cor. 11:1). A maturing son is a pattern son, for he freely relinquishes any claim he has on his personal rights, yielding them to the Elder Son. A maturing son lives to bring honor to Him who was and is and will always be the first in everything. A true son knows that all the Glory belongs to Him forever, and so he freely casts his crown before Him who humbled Himself to transform fallen man into a new creation—the One Who is, in fact, the Ancient of Days.

The Pattern Intercessor

Therefore I will divide Him a portion with the great, and He shall divide the spoil with the strong, because He poured out His soul unto death, and He was numbered with the transgressors, and He bore the sin of many, and made intercession for the transgressors (Isaiah 53:12).

Jesus was and is the consummate intercessor. He knew that apart from His Father He could do nothing. He offered Himself, not just in prayer but in complete surrender to the will of His Father. He knew that His prayers could only result in Himself becoming the answer that He asked His Father to provide.

Because intercession requires attentive listening before anything is actually asked, it more often results in an answer. Usually that answer will come through the one who is the intercessor. Intercession is not merely "praying hard" for something, nor is it "praying long." Intercession is the very heart of our King calling forth the power of eternity to physically alter things as they are in order to bring things into Divine harmony as they should be. Jesus, as the Pattern intercessor, was not content to simply pray for us; He offered Himself as the answer the world so desperately needs. His sons shall be no less.

I once asked God to help a friend with rent money. I ended up writing the check. I once asked God to help a young missionary get to the field. I was the one who bought his ticket. Once I was in Italy where a dedicated, sincere pastor needed a car. I ended up buying the car he needed. It was then that I decided I would limit my prayer just for those who needed less expensive things, like a hat or a pair of gloves! Of course, I am kidding, but the lesson is a serious one. The intercessor very often becomes the answer to the need. In his intercession, the intercessor is offering himself as the conduit for the Divine answer to flow. Intercession is motivated by a love so profound that one cannot help but be the offering that would supply the need, whatever that need might be. The more one is willing to relinquish control over his own body, soul, and spirit, the more effective he will be and the more he will enter into the ministry of the Pattern Intercessor.

The Pattern Son of God, Jesus Christ, interceded in ways we cannot imagine. Whether it was opening blind eyes, feeding the thousands, raising the dead, gathering the children, or taking the sins of the world upon Himself on the Cross, the pattern is clear. Those who are maturing sons offer themselves to become the answer to the prayer they pray, even to the point of laying down our lives as Jesus did for us.

The Pattern Healer

There is no question that the signs and wonders caught the attention of all of ancient Israel and of the Roman government that ruled over them. Jesus was the consummate compassionate one. He was single-minded and focused on the wholeness of the people. The masses ran to Him to experience the miraculous power of this Divine Messenger, this Prophet sent by the Ancient of Days. But His work did not end with the myriad demonstrations of His power. The Pattern Healer did not just heal the body, He healed the soul. He fed them Divine words that brought supernatural comfort and hope. His endgame was not the healing of the lepers, freeing the demoniacs, feeding the thousands, or even raising the dead. His endgame was the restoration of their hearts to their Father. His goal was to not only demonstrate the loving friendship He had with His Father but to teach the people that they, too, could enjoy the same deep, interactive relationship that the Pattern Healer had with His Father.

Contemporary pattern healers carry the same passion, the same desire, the same goal. The healing power they carry is not for a post on the Internet, a video to promote a ministry, or a reason to take an offering. The authentic pattern healer demonstrates the same attributes of the Pattern Healer in every way, with a mindset of true servanthood. His work is for the people to experience the same dynamic of friendship with their Father. The miracles only get their attention so that the Father may get their friendship, devotion, and worship. The maturing son takes no glory unto himself, no opportunity for personal advancement or demand for personal attention. With each healing and miracle, maturing sons are decreasing that He may be, in all ways, increasing. Sons will seize every opportunity to exult the Father. They see every miracle as a testimony that proves the love of the Father. Healers are about only one thing—lifting up the Pattern Son that the Father may be worshiped and His Kingdom established in the hearts of once mere mortal men.

The Pattern Lover

We love Him because He first loved us (1 John 4:19).

There is no greater pattern for a modern believer than to see Him as the Pattern Lover. He loves when others hate. He reaches out His hands to those who close theirs to Him. His love for humanity does not give room to return anything else but what is in Him, no matter what comes to Him from those who reject Him. There is nothing within Him that can be stirred up against those who hate Him because there is nothing but love within Him. The maturing son is learning to be like his Elder

Brother, to surrender the attitudes that can be stirred to respond to unkindness in like manner.

> *And walk in love, as Christ also has loved us and given Himself for us, an offering and a sacrifice to God for a sweet-smelling aroma* (Ephesians 5:2).

There is no doubt that the overriding force in the life of Jesus is His compelling love, His focused compassion toward humanity. I sometimes wonder what John was remembering when he penned the words, "For God so loved the world that He gave His only begotten Son" (John 3:16). For John had witnessed Jesus in His demonstrable love during His earthly ministry. John watched as our Pattern Lover spoke with such gentleness to the masses, forgave their weakness, gathered their children and healed their sick, fed them, and brought the reality of God to the most broken and destitute. I think John was remembering how Jesus stayed with the people for hours on end, ate in their homes, and embraced the worst of sinners. He remembered Jesus' words of hope and love and promise. But it was more than that. My imagination lets me think John, himself, had such an overwhelming vision of his Father as he watched His Son. John witnessed firsthand the limitless flow of Divine favor, Divine love—well, Divine everything through Jesus. Yes, it was what John saw that gave him the confidence to pen those most-quoted words of the New Testament. Yes, God so loved the world that He gave the world His Everything, His Joy, His Only Begotten for the body, soul, and spiritual redemption of all mankind in every age and for all time. Such was the nature, the power, the expression of Father's love through our Pattern Lover.

The Pattern Lover longs to hear the confession that He made concerning His interaction with the enemy of our souls: "for the ruler of this world is coming, and he has nothing in Me" (John 14:30).

The Pattern Expression of His Father

He is the image of the invisible God, the firstborn over all creation (Colossians 1:15).

The life of Jesus was and is the very image of who our Father is. We all love to quote the scripture, "I only do what I see my Father in heaven doing" (see John 5:19), but I doubt that we understand its implications. Many have referenced this verse when teaching about miracles. However, there is a far more important aspect to what Jesus said here. Let's put that verse together with these: "I and My Father are one" (John 10:30), and again, "He who has seen Me has seen the Father" (John 14:9). Nothing could be clearer concerning the desire of our Elder Brother toward His Father. He wanted the world to see the compassionate, loving, forgiving, gentle Father as He truly is. He wanted humanity to know the gracious, gathering, healing heart of His Father the way He already knew Him. Jesus knew that the world, who could not see His Father would judge His Father by the actions, attitudes, and lifestyle of His son.

> *I do not pray for these alone, but also for those who will believe in Me through their word; that they all may be one, as You, Father, are in Me, and I in You; that they also may be one in Us, that the world may believe that You sent Me. And the glory which You gave Me I have given them, that they may be one just as We are one: I in them, and You in Me; that they may be made perfect in one, and that the world may know that You have sent Me, and have loved them as You have loved Me* (John 17:20-23).

What a powerful prayer Jesus prayed—that we would experience Oneness with our Father the way Jesus and His Father were one! What a powerful testimony of the Son's incredible love for His Father that He would want us to know Him as Jesus did. Everything we need to know about the depth of relationship between Jesus and His Father comes out in these few verses. We discover the eternal power and depth of relationship in the Divine by watching the Son and His Father interact. No less is true of us today. The world will gauge our Father by our actions, attitudes, and lifestyle as well.

Therefore, a quiet life of reflection and softness of heart is essential if the world is to see Him as He truly is. For those who want to be the express image of the Son that will draw the world to Him, this is a critical part of the required lifestyle, born of passionate desire for the world to see Him as He truly is.

The Pattern Everything

For our citizenship is in heaven, from which we also eagerly wait for the Savior, the Lord Jesus Christ, who will transform our lowly body that it may be conformed to His glorious body, according to the working by which He is able even to subdue all things to Himself (Philippians 3:20-21).

The transformation of everything began with the Pattern Everything, for He is certainly the manifest example of the loving power of the Divine on earth. For us, this is a mighty shift from primarily earthy things to the Divinely birthed New Creation. It begins with the transformation of the human heart and ends with the fulfillment of the long-awaited plan of God for this planet. As we have seen, this shift is a very real and very permanent. The evidence is proven by the change that is wrought as He works among us. It cannot be duplicated by earthy means as it is not an earthy shift. It is initiated with the Divine and has its completion in the heart of the truly surrendered. There are not enough pages in this book to discuss the full interaction of the human and the Divine in every aspect of life. My conscious participation and co-labor with my Elder Brother will be manifest outwardly in all I say and do, all I write and touch. This transformation will result in the authentic emergence of the King, that He might be seen in us throughout all creation.

> *And as we have borne the image of the man of dust, we shall also bear the image of the heavenly Man* (1 Corinthians 15:49).

The emergence of the sons of God is changing everything, not the least of which is how the world will see Jesus. Who He truly is and His eternal desires for humanity will be made evident. Once this is seen, we shall see the trees of the field clapping their hands as nature's intercession emerges victorious. We will see the highway of holiness crowded with the jubilant rejoicing of the Redeemed, the complete fulfillment of Jesus' final words, "It is finished." Then will Micah's vision come to pass in time and space:

> *And it will come about in the last days that the mountain of the house of the Lord will be established as the chief of the mountains. It will be raised above the hills, and the peoples will stream to it. Many nations will come and say, "Come and let us go up to the mountain of the Lord and to the house of the God of Jacob, that He may teach us about His ways and that we may walk in His paths." For from Zion will go forth the law, even the word of the Lord from Jerusalem* (Micah 4:1-2 NASB).

Questions for the Transforming Son

1. Do you spend time meditating on the nature and character of Jesus Christ? If you do, how has this changed you?

2. How does it make you feel that the world's understanding of the Father is through you and I? Does it change how you see yourself relating to others?

3. Are you confident in His ability to bring you into maturity and fullness?

There Is No Last Chapter

I Know Your Heart

I know who you are, my dear reader, because I know your heart. Your heart is just like mine. We all know that this book is not the end of the journey. It is not the sum total of all there to know and experience as a maturing son. It is but a sliver of what your Father and mine has prepared for us. It is a brief glimpse of what our Elder Brother has accomplished and demonstrated for us as He walked the earth and now walks the rooms of our hearts. He is still doing His work of Kingdom building within us and ultimately in all of creation.

I am sure there will be other books and other writers (maybe you) who will see more, experience more, and touch more of Him than I have ever hoped for. I am also certain that you will need to surrender even further so that His discernment, wisdom, and witness will be your guides as you continue to walk through life on this most amazing and wonderful sojourn with our King.

The good news at the end of this book is simple. The book has come to an end but the journey continues. There is no final chapter. Transformation is an exhilarating lifelong experience. I know that as long as I breathe, I will always discover deeper opportunities to surrender to His will and experience more of His eternal Life right here on this planet. The world's claim on my life grows weaker with each surrender. Paradoxically, my hiddenness in Him becomes more visible with each passing day as He increases in influence, love, and power within me. By His grace I will yield to Him. And when I fail to relinquish control to Him, I am certain that His unfailing love and compassion will gather me once again to His heart in complete assurance that I will win again.

Yes, I know your heart. I know your heart because I know my own heart and I know the heart of the King. They all beat with the same passion, the same love, the same determination. You and I are walking this path together with Him. It is an adventure as perilous as any mountain climb, exhilarating as any morning sunrise, and as risky as a skydive. For if we are courageous and willing, this journey will lead us to clearer understanding of His ways, renewing us from the small thoughts of mortal man to the eternal thoughts of God Himself. The conclusion to all of this will be the authentic and permanent transformation of our inner man. The nations will run to our King when they see Him as He really is, through you and me. It is to this end that I dedicate myself each morning, and why I have written this book.

I am certain that when I breathe my last breath, the attitude of my heart, if not the last words I ever utter, will be, "I surrender to You, my King, my Lord, my Master, my Captain, my Friend, and my Brother." For as He is the Firstborn Son, so I AM also a son, and so are you. After all, I know your heart.

And every creature which is in heaven and on the earth and under the earth and such as are in the sea, and all that are in them, I heard saying: "Blessing and honor and glory and power be to Him who sits on the throne, and to the Lamb, forever and ever!" (Revelation 5:13)

About Don Nori, Sr.

Don Nori, Sr. is a driven man. The same passion for Jesus that arrested him over 40 years ago is the passion that led him to start Destiny Image Publishers in 1983 and is still the primary overshadowing power in his life today. Along with Cathy, his wife of more than 43 years, they pursue life enthusiastically in the beautiful Cumberland Valley of central Pennsylvania. They spend much of their time happily spoiling their grandchildren and enjoying their sons and their wives. Don will probably write as long as God gives him breath.

BOOKS FOR MATURING SONS

Forgotten Mountain

The Voice

The God Watchers

Romancing the Divine

FREE E-BOOKS?
YES, PLEASE!

Get **FREE** and deeply discounted **Christian books** for your **e-reader** delivered to your inbox **every week!**

IT'S SIMPLE!

VISIT lovetoreadclub.com

SUBSCRIBE by entering your email address

RECEIVE free and discounted e-book offers and inspiring articles delivered to your inbox every week!

Unsubscribe at any time.

SUBSCRIBE NOW!

LOVE TO READ CLUB

visit **LOVETOREADCLUB.COM** ▶

www.ingramcontent.com/pod-product-compliance
Lightning Source LLC
Chambersburg PA
CBHW060535100426
42743CB00009B/1533